PUBLISHED *by* PARABLES
Earthly Stories with a Heavenly Meaning

Parenting Beyond Tragedy

PARENTING
BEYOND TRAGEDY

A MALE PERSPECTIVE
DAMON L. DAVIS

PUBLISHED by PARABLES
Earthly Stories with a Heavenly Meaning

Parenting Beyond Tragedy

Parenting Beyond Tragedy
Damon L. Davis

Published By Parables
April, 2022

Printed in the United States of America

Readers should be aware that Internet Web sites offered as citations and/or sources for further information may have been changed or disappeared between the time this was written and the time it is read.

PARENTING

BEYOND TRAGEDY

A MALE PERSPECTIVE

DAMON L. DAVIS

PUBLISHED by PARABLES
Earthly Stories with a Heavenly Meaning

Parenting Beyond Tragedy

Eulogy: **Redemption**

Son, if you only knew how you changed me. Challenged me, pushed me away. Made me question feeling discouraged. Defeated. Was I made for this? Cut out for you? Where did I go wrong? Where did I fail you, son? Never wanted to hurt you. Disappoint you Everything was for you. I missed the mark. I'm sorry. Trying to make it up. You make me proud. And you're so strong, intelligent, creative, thoughtful. I did something right. God has a plan for you. He trusted me. I never gave up, never will. You are called, by Him. The head and not the tail. Created in his image. He will give you beauty for ashes. Make crooked ways straight. You are forgiven So am I. Let's walk forward, Together......

Redemption.

by Lisa M. Phillips.

Parenting Beyond Tragedy

"No other success can compensate for the failure in the home. Truly, the work you do within your own home is the greatest work you will ever do. The family is of supreme importance and deserves more time and attention than we traditionally give it. People will spend hundreds of hours thinking through a detailed strategy at work but then won't bother to spend a few hours planning how to build a stronger family."

~ Excerpt from a final interview with **Stephen R. Covey author of "7 Habits of Highly Effective People"**

Parenting Beyond Tragedy

Damon L. Davis

This book is dedicated to my lovely mother who is triumphant as a single parent over all the abuse suffered to provide for me, my sister, and my older brother and also for being victorious in forbearing the agony of this tragedy; the incarceration of her youngest son.

And also, to my daughters Lavie Renee-Carter, Cayline Purcell, and Maraia Lynnmnik Davis the most precious gifts in my life. I am deeply sorry for robbing us of the experience of growing, learning, knowing, and loving one another.

Parenting Beyond Tragedy

Damon L. Davis

Special Acknowledgements

To the Single Mother's
Parents Beyond Tragedy

Ahmed Nelms' Jameye Myres

And to My:
Aunt Kathy Abernathy
Sister Ametrius Tatina Ellis
Sister Latasha Hamm
Lil Cousin Kia Abernathy
Dear friend Lisa M. Phillips
Dear friend and 'kindred spirit'
Megan Krutsche

I'm forever Grateful to: My soul supporters in every occasion in every instance.

Ms. Clementine Pigford, *(rest in paradise)*. I am deeply saddened that I never got to say goodbye. I am so very grateful for all the roles you took the time to be, for me.

Mindee Mitchell-Brown, I never thought that so much fearlessness could be found in such a kind spirited person. You had the courage when no one else did and you used it to enrich the lives of us who dared to challenge ourselves to be better. I am wealthier in life because of you.

Ms. Carla Woods, 'Detroit's Finest', you are the essence of sisterhood, family, culture, legacy, and compassion. A ball of fire when called upon to stand firm for what you believe in, for yourself and others.

THANK YOU ALL! "You are my evidence that there are angels in every aspect of life; in heaven and hell on earth, in freedom and captivity. God's reach is far beyond the reach of our one-dimensional senses and comprehension."

Damon L. Davis

A Special Dedication

Jayden Lee Phillips
(March 13th,2003-October 18th, 2021)
"May you rest in Paradise. I love you and I miss you.
Thank for being in my life. You are an inspiration."

To all the families and children impacted by domestic
violence, the cycle of mass incarceration, and the
incomprehensible tragedy of violent crime.

Parenting Beyond Tragedy

Preface

Parenting beyond Tragedy, a male's perspective is about parenting and co-parenting through situations that are emotionally traumatizing for children; such as divorce, parental suicide, or the untimely death of one or both parents, incarceration of one or both parents, and children that experience adoption agencies.

Co- parenting means to promote the overall healthiest possible parenting culture for the wellbeing of the child or children involved in these situations. What's in the best interest of the child', as we've all heard it stated by many child service & social agencies and courts alike. Yet, upon closer observation of that statement, that's not always the case. It should more likely read, "what's in the best interest of the (mother) of the child."

Unwittingly or otherwise, society has created a standard for women (i.e. mother's in such circumstances as described above) to be tyrannical- dictators toward the fathers in these situations; the mothers portraying themselves as the victims / caretakers of the children, where much of the focus and energy is spent indignantly trying to deprive the father of something instead of what's truly ethical and empathetically in the best interest of the child; the children who are of course, the only true victims in parental disputes, divorce, foster care, and unexpected tragedies such as incarceration that separate children from their parents.

For purposes of this book we will focus on the subject of the incarceration of a parent (i.e. the father) thus, the male's perspective.

This book will also introduce experiences from two other incarcerated fathers' author Mr. William S. Graham and Mr. Ahmad Nelms. I have had the privilege speaking with a variety of men from different races and walks of life on this subject. I was only able to get these two men to share their experiences on paper.

I want to make clear that this book is not an attack on women, or the many great single mothers' out there holding it down for their children whose fathers are incarcerated. This is however, a brazen effort to give men a voice in an otherwise female dominated arena. In addition to being a call to action for dialog about the important role the male presence plays in the family structure, upbringing, and overall well being of his children. This is (all) in the name of what's truly in the best interest of the child.

I will address the importance of the male role preferably, the biological father and why his presence in any form is still vital to the development of the child's mental and emotional health especially when his physical presence is not possible. That-That space, when properly cultivated is very relevant as to having (both) parents in the child's life as much as possible when tragedy strikes (as in the best-case scenario) vs. only one parent struggling to make sense of it all for the children's sake. Let alone when the father's efforts are completely emasculated in the eyes of his children for the baby momma's sake in wake of losing the father to the penitentiary.

There seems to be a societal notion that has spread into an epidemic among families, couples, and singles that strongly suggests to women that it is excusable to exclude the biological father from the parenting process altogether whenever they feel that circumstances are no longer ideal for themselves. The mother 's feelings toward the father are of little importance where the child's best interest is concerned. At that point, 'what's in the best interest of the child' is an after thought, a second-row seat to her volatile feelings and emotional state. Nevertheless, the mother's position is the position that's reinforced by society and the custody courts alike. My intention is to restore balance on this sensitive issue that has gone un-touched and unspoken of for too long from the male's perspective. No two parents are perfect. Parenting is an un-masterful art. My approach is one of non-avoidance, simple and direct. I believe that the path

to healing is by confronting the pain and deal with the difficult situations. After all, life is difficult. Life is challenging. It is what it is. This book embodies the true essence of what it means to (ACT) in the BEST interest of the child in healthiest way possible when tragedy strikes.

In order to address this epidemic objectively, honestly and transparently I am calling your attention at what I call 'The Sins' of both parents. By 'sin' I mean the core and basic responsibility of each parent no matter the circumstances; responsibilities that become a sin when we act out of accordance, neglect, or behave with extreme indifference to them. Yet I am also introducing the *antidote*. Like raw medicine, the taste is not so great but the effects are ideal for healing the ailment, the family structure, the broken home (*parenting beyond tragedy*). I hope that this approach is something we all can stomach in the quest to begin healing the wounds; by universal accountability and straight forwardness because parenting, in and of itself is one of life's most beautiful

challenges; a gift of joyful and unpredictable magnitudes in which we are all forever students in an un-masterful arena.

Forward

A moment of silence please for: Jayden Lee Phillips tragically killed October 18th, 2021. He was 18 years old. His mother's eldest son. He thought of me as an Uncle. His mother Lisa and I have been friends for 25 years.

Lisa writes:
Thank you for taking the time to pour into my son. You have made an impact and have been consistent and that is so important to him. I hope he has impacted you as well. I just wanted to say I appreciate you and your efforts.

I am glad you got a chance to talk to him on the phone while he was out. He was glad that happened as well.

Again, I appreciate you pouring knowledge and wisdom in him while he was here. He needed that love.

-Love Always, your friend Lisa

Parenting Beyond Tragedy

Introduction:
The Universe Paused
The universe paused, darkness falls, and you came into the light in spite of it all.
Specifically chosen, woven with perfection, a sensual selection of the female anatomy, 'our baby', unaware of the fragile structure of your mommy and me.

The Universe Paused
You were God's gift, our responsibility; 'you', a divine blessing to the entire family. I christened thee; still they tried selfishly to separate you from me. Ironically, in light of my mistakes it seems I helped them succeed effortlessly. And though I'm a go-hard, give my all type of dad. None of it truly matters in the wake of this tragedy. Still I can't ever recall missing a 'Merry Christmas or Happy Birthday' whether by letter or with Angel Tree. They say that actions speak louder than words. I suppose mine were never felt.

The Universe paused
You're a teen. You're angry. You're unable to reach me. I understand empathetically and I have always taken full responsibility and accountability for the imperfect me. And even though it kills me, I've never once drowned in self-pity. I've stood up strong under my burdens with God's mercy reaching out to my baby. So how is it that you don't know me nor can recollect one pleasant memory? Sadly, your mom never told you all the great things about me. For your benefit or hers, think about it

seriously. Where's the transparency if it was never really about her and me?

The Universe Paused
You are a young adult with children now,
Yeah…It's alright baby. Spread your wings. Be free. We wouldn't be the first generation whose fruit fell so far away from the tree. So just promise me, that upon delivery you'll kiss my grandson for me, make up the perfect story in hopes he'll start a new legacy based on what he doesn't know about me.

"My foundation, my history, my family," the dynamic three, his history, how would any of it be possible without communicating?

The Universe Paused

BOOM!

Parenting Beyond Tragedy.

Prolog

mistakes as a father come from the same root as described by author William S. Graham in 'Hurt People Hurt people' where he talks about generational trauma as well as isolated trauma being passed on from person to person (i.e. relationships, marriages, from parents to children, and even unhealthy friendships etc. etc.). Of course, this isn't a new term or topic for anyone who is familiar with the deeper roots of trauma. Like wise, for me this process began way before I ever thought about having children of my own. From my own parental mistakes as well as, from my own upbringing I learned that parents under duress are less sensitive and less tentative to a child's other talents and creativity beyond their general education and basic needs; food, shelter, and clothing. Those necessities soon become the essentials and only make up one third of the child's over all wellbeing. A child's mental, emotional health and education are the other key factors that

help ensure a child's success. Yet, many families that are operating under such duress due to impoverished-violent environments, low-social economic status, or suffering from traumatizing experiences often lack the proper coping skills and resources to perform thru these challenges at an optimum level. Therefore, as individuals, as parents, we can only give what we have; out of lack, springs forth more lacking despite our best intentions and efforts. This doesn't negate the love, care, concern, and desire to want the best for our children nor does it severe the child-parent connection. But it does create gaps in the communication. In some cases, the struggle may deepen the parent-child bond, in other's it may cripple it. Nevertheless, even the strongest parent-child bond would not negate the unaddressed impact of psychological trauma suffered from generation to generation. A cycle, ignored by prochoice or by self-absolving denial that may go on forever in such circumstances. And in some extreme cases may only be addressed, if ever, and set on a journey of healing by external sources, as in an intervention with others (from the outside looking in). Sadly, this is the only time some of us seriously self-reflect. Then the other scenario, is when a compounded tragedy or melee tough issues of circumstance and poor choices causes one to re-evaluate one's life. That person, by their own volition has taken up the courageous and difficult task of looking themselves in the mirror most honestly and often in order to redirect their lives. In any event, someone has to WAKE UP!

I am not suggesting that circumstances are an excuse to make poor decisions. I am implying that once a person becomes aware of a solution to a problem, as well as, one's error in a given situation; that circumstances no matter how unpleasant, difficult, well, or otherwise is no excuse to ignore, deny, nor avoid the necessary steps needed to resolve the issue. Even the rich, the noblest, most ethical, are prone to the most devastating human error when we are overwhelmed with stress, emotionally intoxicated and unequipped under such duress to make sober decisions. The effects of a bad criminal decision as a parent can have crippling consequences on the family *unit. Particularly for people such as myself, where my* mistakes have landed me in prison for decades of time; it can create an irreparable gap between parent and child. Despite the damage, I feel that an attempt at reconciliation must be made on my part, no matter what. I made the mistake not my children. It is a painful and very difficult process. Nevertheless, this is where my legacy minds set-sets in. It is my belief, it doesn't matter when or when a person finally wakes up; the goal is to stop the cycle at all cost. So, here, in this space, as an incarcerated father I acknowledge the source of (my) folly and address it head on.

"WE MUST EMANCIPATE OURSELVES FROM MENTAL SLAVERY." –Bob Marley

The starting point of the healing process of any wound usually hurts. So, in light of the above quote we must begin with ourselves. Such scrutiny will require raw and honest reflection into the dark and painful corners of our own thoughts, actions, and behaviors. Reflections that we are usually in extreme denial about when forced to look at ourselves in the mirror. I mean, let's face it, no one wants to admit that they failed at something; especially when that 'something' *is close to the heart that you tenderly had hoped to succeed at.*

Parenting Beyond Tragedy

Chapter 1: **Imperfect Picture**
In order to understand me, Damon Lee Davis, the man, and the circumstances that brought me to prison, you would first have to understand that, before I was an absentee father, and before I was a convicted felon; I was a child myself.

From the very moment that I witnessed the abuse of my mother I became the child who internalized his mother's pain. Emotionally and psychologically, I began to take on every other problem in the family. I felt it was my responsibility to make my mother happy, ease her pain, and make my family whole again. From that experience as a boy I became relentless in my will to succeed. My pain and confusion were released with a fierce spirit to win in the form of healthy and maybe unhealthy competition with myself and others. I felt like I needed to be somebody that could change our circumstances and I wasn't going to let anyone tear me down or stop me from succeeding at that. For example, I was the type of kid that if you punched me; I punched you ten times as much. If you challenged me to a foot race, I'd smoke you. If you were faster than me, cool, you'd have to race me until you couldn't run anymore. It was the norm with me with pretty much everything from ridding wheelies on a tenth-speed with no hands, to back flips, sports, and even with academics. I was highly competitive. But when it came to school, I did well only when I was able to focus on the subjects at hand my grades were above average. When I was distracted by things at home my grades slipped dramatically. Suppressing my emotions hurt my performance in school. Yet, my spirit was unbreakable. I was always hustling even as a young kid. From age nine I cut grass, raked leaves, collected cans, and shoveled snow all season long. At the age of ten I built a little shack out of old wood from our back yard. I bought candy from the 'Q.T.' (Quick Trip) and sold it from the shack. The shack was also a mini club house for me and my friends. At age twelve, my uncles Harold and Gary taught me how to cut hair. So, whenever we were at granny's house in Rock Hill. I ended up cutting dang near all the kids' hair we knew in our neighborhood. My first cousin Hasani was my most loyal customer. Of course, he didn't have to pay a penny. Yet, he did have to suffer all of my beginner mistakes along the way. But without Hasani I never would have gotten so good so fast. That was me as a boy.

Now, as a teenager around the age of fifteen. We were forced (by circumstances) to leave St. Louis. We landed here in Colorado. (This was before me and my older brother Marvin got separated) there was another level of pain that settled into my spirit. The pain of watching my mother struggle as a single parent to provide for me and my siblings. Mom would rarely eat. Whenever she did eat of course, she made sure that we ate first. This was difficult for me for several reasons. One, because I knew mom was just as hungry as we were. Two, I could see how the stress of everything was breaking mom down physically, she was becoming much thinner than she use to be in a very short time. And three, I just felt guilt eating while mom ate very little or at all. Us kids, had voracious appetites, especially me. I was hyper-sensitive to my mother's feeling and emotions. I could always sense her sadness or frustration. Additionally, I was a hyper teen, I couldn't sit still very long and I didn't sleep well. It's a trip as an adult looking back on all this, knowing what I know now about my health and just other knowledge in general. I didn't know about hyper or hypothyroidism back then, but it wouldn't surprise me if I had it then.

Mom worked nights and the refrigerator was always good the first two weeks after pay day. The rent was paid and mom was great at budgeting. Yet, with three mouths
besides her own, things were a bit difficult. It was the last two weeks of the month before the next payday that were the hardest. We were just some hungry ass kids. Mom was single, very prideful, and independent (not to mention very stubborn). She was determined to do it without food stamp assistance. So, it was rough. She did it on her own. Still, with three hungry mouths to feed, two of them, very active teenage boys (just two-years apart), and one girl it was challenging. She worked late. Even though her shift ended at 11p.m., she wouldn't get home till like 12 a.m. some nights. So, we were accustomed to staying up very late at night. There were nights that mom stopped by the store on the way home and would bring unexpected snacks and stuff. Especially if it was one of those long weeks when food was low. On the night's mom worked and we were short on ramen, the three of us split what was there. If there wasn't enough for all three of us our older brother would let me and my younger sister eat. There were times when we were out of ramen and there were only potatoes. We'd fry them in butter (even the skins). Still after making whatever

servings of fries between us, we were still hungry. Marvin would rock his hunger pains away by laying on the floor of our unfurnished apartment listening to his Walkman. Music was his escape (*pretty soon he'd have an even better escape*). Meanwhile, hungry and restless I'd sneak out of the apartment window to shoplift from the nearby Albertson's. They often left cases of pop, and watermelons (to my surprise); even Tostitos' stacked right outside the store. I was shocked. You'd never see anything like that in St. Louis except for watermelons and pumpkins. These were just some of the many experiences that shaped my mentality at an early age. Even then, I possessed the instinct to find solutions when things weren't going so great. They weren't always the best solutions, but I didn't just sit around, my mind was constantly working. I did my best to try to find a way out of no way. I thank god for my mind state.

If you were looking at my life from the outside looking in, as a coach or scouting agent I'd probably look like the next up and coming star athlete. From a business man's point of view, you'd most likely coin me as a natural born entrepreneur/business owner; or a possible protégé. These are observations that could have turned out great for me and my family in the long run. I was a naturally talented and gifted young man. Yet, parents don't always have the time to focus and help their children cultivate these gifts. So, to my mother who was swimming in an ocean storm of her own pain and struggle; I imagine she saw just another one of her children whom she loved dearly that she would go to any lengths to protect and provide for. Which she did, through sheer determination and hard work. It was from her that I learned not to allow myself to be shrunken by circumstances. Of course, the wisdom of her example came later in my life. However, my mom was my first true role model. As for how the school districts and the Colorado Springs police department viewed me…I'm sure all they saw was a mischievous-troubled teen that needed to be controlled, disciplined, eradicated, or all the above. And it didn't matter which came first.

Parenting Beyond Tragedy

Chapter 2: **Pain in St. Louis Missouri**
It wasn't long after we moved from the Kinloch to Smithfield Road into a house for the first time that the arguments and abuse began again with my mom and my step-dad. Jerry was a drinker and they would always argue late at night. My siblings and I often heard the fights and thing s breaking, but this night was different. I heard, "Jerry stop! Stop it Jerry, Jerry please, oh my knee, Jerry no!" As my mother lay on the floor crying, clutching her knee. "Momma," I said. "Its okay baby, go back to bed," she replied. (Jerry had gone into the kitchen before storming out of the house). All the while, my older brother and younger sister remained in their rooms through it all. For my mother, it was the last straw. She had already suffered a deep a cut on her face from shattered glass Jerry broke by punching it while she stood behind it one day. (*At 65, my mom still requires a knee brace from time to time and the scar from the stitches on her left cheek are still visible*)**.**

(*It's a horrific thing to witness someone harming your mother, our step dad, a man we all loved*). At age nine, I learned that fear, hurt, confusion, and anger created tightness in my chest that was only released by tears that no one saw; feeling helpless to protect my mother that day. I had failed as a child and as the years passed, I still felt helpless to help heal her hurts. Soon after the attack on my mother it was back to Rock Hill, back to granny's house, my moms' mom.

1987

At granny's house. Initially it was me, Hasani, Marvin, Meechie, Kathy, my mom, and granny. I don't know how granny remained so calm and regal with all of us living there. It was crowded but it was home and it was safe. However, short-lived. (Fleeing her abuser, my mom had a plan that included getting all of us out of St. Louis altogether. A plan she eventually executed in stages.) My brother and had no intention of leaving St. Louis. For the time being things were peaceful. Yet, it was only a matter of time before I saw one of my favorite aunts with a black eye. We were close and to be honest we were all shocked. My first cousin Hasani was her only child. Kathy was the aunt with all the spunk. She didn't take any shit from anyone. And she was always full of positive energy. She didn't treat me any different than my brother or my sister, but she always had a way of making you feel special when she spoke to you. The magic was in her tone of voice. I felt like she loved me more than everyone. (*Selfish, I know. I was a kid*). But, she made me feel like I was her favorite little person in the whole world. So, I was hurt and extremely pissed when I saw my aunts' eye. Everyone was upset. There wasn't a male presence in the home; only women and children. Hasani was two years younger than me. He was hurt and pissed that-that fool had the nerve to hit his momma. I could sense that he felt that he was too young; that any of us were too young to do anything. But, I was plotting and I made no secret about it. I hugged Hasani and I promised my cousin that I would get Kelvin one day. Marvin was the eldest at 14 years old. (*he was mad too, though I'm not sure how all of this affected my older*

30

brother. He didn't express much but I know for a fact, that it did bother him though he internalized all the drama differently. When things got to the point where he felt he might do something. Marvin's would go across the street to his friend Kevin's house). So, when we all witnessed aunt Kathy with a black eye; for some odd reason I felt it was on me to protect us. I don't know what I could have actually did to a grown man, but I would have figured something out (*I loved baseball and there were plenty of bats around the house*). None of us liked Kelvin. We all saw past his act. As soon as we saw Kathy's eye we all knew who did it. We hated him now, for three reasons. For starters he was always cussing at my aunt and being aggressive with her in front us kids and granny. Two, he was the reason my aunt started using and got hooked on drugs and three, he finally put his hands on her; leaving a wound that we could all see. I was furious as a kid. Hitting my aunt was like hitting my mother. I was only twelve at the time, but I swore to my aunt that I was going to get him one day. Hasani had told her what I said. So, she believed me to. I started keeping my baseball bat with me everywhere I went like Linus and his blanket on Charlie brown. Kelvin knew it too. When he came by he was only allowed to step foot on the porch. I made sure he always saw me with my bat. I would kneel on a chair in the window with my bat under my chin while they spoke outside. And when he sat in a car waiting for Kathy to come outside, I sat or stood on the porch with my bat. I wasn't going to sit back idle if he struck my aunt again. Then Kathy became pregnant by him we we're devastated we were all thinking the same thing (*like, now we will never be rid of him*). You could see it written all over my grandmother's face. But the truth, in spite of our feelings, was that Hasani was going to have a baby sister and Kelvin was the father. This was the saga, all the while, my mother was having a nervous breakdown. We didn't see her much during that transition. She took a brief two hiatus; staying with other relatives. It was mainly to keep us safe while she went and worked things out with Jerry. She heard him out and listened to his story. (*In all aspects, Jerry was a good guy. He was good to us. Though he was the biological father of only our sister he treated my brother and I, all the same. I have a lot of fond memories with him. His problem was drinking and whatever relationship issues he and our mom shared. Unfortunately for him, when it came to the physical abuse, my mom wasn't having it*). This was the breaking point for mom. And in our minds, she was really tripping. She kept saying that everyone was against her meaning other family members and that we were leaving. She wanted to move to Colorado. My brother Marvin and I weren't with that idea. (*Me and my brother had the same mother & father*). Our dad's sister's aunt *Mary*, aunt *Phyllis*, and aunt *Gracie* (*rest in paradise*) had been in Colorado Springs since the early eighties. Along with our cousins Eric, Demetrius, Christopher, and Danielle. My brother and I had visited before when we were younger. It felt like a paradise compared to St. Louis, we loved it, but we weren't with the whole, "let's pack up and move to Colorado thing." St. Louis was our home. Mom was unstable and tripping hard, so Kathy and granny told all the kids to stay in the house till things blew over. Which really just meant, "Otha's kids." Me, Marvin, and Meechie. We couldn't even go to the park unless we all went together which was crazy because we were all different ages; we did not play together. To me and my younger sister Meechie it felt like a forever punishment. We were young. For our older brother Marvin, it meant that he could still go to Kevin's, at least he couldn't be seen and swooped up by mom. And for our cousin Hasani it meant nothing. His outside privileges were never at stake. Hasani was my first cousin we were around the same age. He was more like my brother than my cousin we were always together. Marvin did his own thing. Nevertheless, Hasani and I convinced Aunt Kathy to let us go to the park. But only if Meechie came with us. She warned us to be careful because Otha Lee, my mom was threatening to take us on a one-way trip from Saint Louis to Colorado (*Mom did not care how unprepared we were over all, she just wanted to leave*). We agreed to be careful. So, Marvin went to his friend Kevin's house. Hasani and I went to play basketball at the bottom of the hill (*the park had two levels*) while Meechie played in the sand by the swings up top. In between games Hasani ran back to the house to grab something. He came back running and saying that Otha Lee just snatched Meechie from the sand box at the park (*we were supposed to be watching her*). And literally, from the park to the high way mom never stopped driving until she reached Colorado. We found out later, from Kathy that they got stranded in Independence Missouri. Mom lost everything. She had to abandon the car at some shop it was towed to with all their belongings. But they eventually arrived in Colorado Springs safe and sound. My brother and I didn't see our mother or sister till a few years later when we were forced to move to Colorado. Angry and confused my brother and I entered **_Colorado Springs in Late 1989._** Several months after arriving my brother and I got word from aunt Phyllis that our father was in Colorado Springs on his way back to California. It was our dad Wesley, his wife Brenda (*Latasha 's mother*), and our sister Latasha. We got in contact with him and gave him the address to where we were. On the day that they were hitting the highway and while our mother was at work in Denver; my brother and I jumped in the Ryder moving truck heading straight for San Diego California. Mom didn't find out till much later. She raised hell when she came home from work to find that we had left our little sister Meechie with the neighbors (*good neighbors that our mom knew and trusted; the superintendent & his family actually*) and hopped in a Ryder truck on a one-way ticket to California. Our mom was pissed, but even more so, she was hurt. (*Okay, maybe she was more pissed than hurt*). Because she reported our father to the police for kidnapping. However, it was a short-lived custody battle that never made it to a court room. My brother and I spoke with the authorities, social services, and our mom. (*Which was a hard for me because I felt like I was abandoning my mom after all she was already going through. And part of me was angry with her because I never wanted to leave (home), St. Louis in the first place*). Marvin was about to turn seventeen and I was almost fifteen. We chose to leave Colorado Springs. We weren't kidnapped. We were with our biological father. So, after all the legal back and forth drama was over we got to stay in California. So, we settled in for school. After visiting the schools within our district and respective grade levels. My brother attended Point Loma High. In California high school begins in ninth grade. I went to was Correa Cougars junior high. My experience was a little challenging and somewhat intimidating. I was not use to being responsible for changing classes on my own recognizance and navigating the compound without a guide. I was use to indoor hallways and pretty much a self-explanatory map of what classes were which and when to go them. Here in California at the new school things were a lot different. The classes were running hourly on a faint bell tone system sort of like the sound you would experience in a hearing test. If you weren't exactly accustomed to it you'd miss it. You would find yourself sitting in the same seat that was once science class instantly converted in to math class. (*It was getting you ready for the actual way high school and colleges were*). Still, it was confusing for me at the time. Only a few months into the semester I wasn't functioning optimally. My grades were slipping; I seemed to only be able to focus in gym class. Marvin on the other hand seemed to be doing quite well. He was better at internalizing things I guess. He was focused and determined to graduate high school and join the military. I remember him saying so, as we toured his then, potential high school the day he enrolled. Marvin did just that. He graduated and joined the U. S. Marine Core stationed right there in San Diego. Me, I was homesick. I mentioned it to my brother and spoke with my dad about how I was feeling. (*I really wanted to go back home to St. Louis, but that wasn't an option. I could only go back to mom in Colorado Springs*). My dad said it was up to me what I wanted to do, but that I need to decide before next semester began. In California, I was unable to adjust well enough to maintain good grades in school. Emotionally, I was messed up. So, I chose back to go back Colorado to be with my mother and sister. And so, for my brother and I, our separate journeys began. It was almost a decade before we saw one another again. #EMOTIONAL RESIDUE

Damon L. Davis

Chapter 3: **A portrait of a fifteen-year-old boy, the man of the house**.

Back in Colorado it was me, my mom, and my baby sister Ametrius. At first, we lived near Sabin junior high where I enrolled. It was a single level school with off-campus lunch privileges. It was a cool bonus because pretty much everything was in walking distance (7-11, a Safeway, a sub-sandwich shop, and two pizza places, one that I loved because they sold single slices. I don't remember the name of it though. The other one was a Red Top restaurant). There were other stores also, the whole little area was kind of a strip mall. Any ways, I wasn't amped about going to school anywhere in Colorado. I was home sick from the very beginning. I just felt out of place. It was a first day at a new school, all eyes were on me. Which wasn't *all that bad*, there were a lot of pretty girls. Girls that I wasn't use to seeing in St. Louis. There were predominately white girls, but also, Asians, and Mexican girls. Still, I got the awkward looks and before long it was all out war on the new kid, or so they thought. As usual, I didn't start fights. Yet, I was nobody's victim. Eventually, the schools' golden boy tested the limits one afternoon and pushed me into the locker as I was attempting to open it (*he found out the hard way that what I lacked in size I packed in heart*). When one teacher pushed through the crowd to see what the commotion was about the other kid was shuffling to his feet. The on-lookers were stunned. And so was I, *when someone yelled out, "Brian started it!" "He pushed him first," said another person.* We were both ushered off to the principal's office. The principal said that because it was my second time coming to his office in two weeks that my mom had to be called. I knew my mom was at work. I sat silent outside the office on a bench till she arrived. The other kid was already in with the principal and gone by the time my mom came. When she saw me, she asked me what happened and I told her. We entered the principal's office together. I sat while they discussed the issue of the fight and why it was so serious that she had to be called. The principal began his case about how this infraction came in the wake of a previous visit where I was kicked out of social studies class for refusing to sing 'The Pledge Allegiance to the Flag' (*The teacher began class every morning by having all the students put their hand over their hearts while singing 'The Pledge of Allegiance'. When asked why I was not participating? I stated, "My mother works for the government, has two jobs and we're still struggling, I don't believe in the American Flag because it doesn't believe in us*). The principal continued to express his reservations about having a kid like me attend his school with that kind of attitude. When the smoke cleared I was expelled. (*Never mind that all my grades were good and I was doing exceptionally well in 'woods-tech'. I actually loved that class. And not to mention that there was supposed to be a three-suspension rule before a child's expulsion from school*). He jumped right past that. My mom wasted no time calling his unjust methods to account demanding some sort of due process. By this time, I was asked to sit outside and whatever those options were didn't matter. My mom was upset, and felt just as discriminated against as I did. We left and she decided that we were better off finding me another school. *(the crazy thing about it all was that the principal was black and also from St. Louis)*. Eventually, we moved out of that district further up north to North Academy and Flintridge to The Russell Junior High school district where I began getting into more trouble. Though I made friends at Russell. I still kept in touch with some of the friends I had when we lived in the Sabin Junior High District. I was sent to juvenile detention at Zebulion Pike for 'theft by receiving' stolen property and harassment. Both incidents happened on school grounds. I brought a camcorder to school one morning; filming everyone having fun, doing all sorts things. I went to off campus lunch leaving it with another student who ended up getting caught for causing too much disruption with it. When he was asked where he got it he said that he'd gotten it from me. When I arrived back at school I was called immediately to the office where two police officers were waiting. They questioned me about where I'd gotten the camcorder from because it was stolen from a home more than a few districts away. There was nothing connecting me to the actual theft or burglary of the home, but since I refused to say where or whom I'd gotten it from I was charged with 'theft by receiving'. My mom was notified. I was suspended; arrested on the spot and taken directly to Zebulion Pike. I spent 45 days in detention for that incident. Once out, I was back at Russel. The harassment occurred just after school ended. I was hanging around with some kids that still actively attended Russell. We were coming from the gym walking down the hall on our way out of the building. There was a student just closing up his locker for the day that the other kids decided they wanted to play a joke on. They wanted to scare him by acting like they wanted something from him. I was game and took the lead role. I thought it would be funny to see the look of fright on the kids face as well. (*in my mind it was funny to me because of how gullible the kids out here were*). So, when I was handed a pocket knife it only added to the play. I told the kid to hold up his arm. I pointed the knife at his armpit (*without touching him*) and said, "Do you want a chicken arm?" We all busted out laughing. Even the kid cracked a smile. It was such a stupid question I thought for sure it gave way to the fact that we were joking all along. The student wasn't harmed nor was any of his belongings ever taken. We never intended on taking anything from him nor harming him, it was a joke. But it never occurred to us, especially not to me, that the kid might actually have been terrified. I didn't think much of it at the time, none of us did. We were still laughing about how scared the kid looked initially. I handed the knife back to the person it belonged to. He went home. A few of us were still hanging around the school yard when the patrol car showed up. Apparently, the kid we played the joke on made it home in time for his mother to hear the story and call the police. She didn't think it was funny nor that it was a joke. We were all question and pat searched for the knife. I was being a smart-ass when the officer asked about the knife. I retorted that it belonged to Moe, Larry, and Curly and they were long gone by now. The policeman was stern and quickly set me straight about being a smart-ass. Still, he seemed to listen to our story that we were just playing around. None of us could really see how everything escalated so fast to this point, but there we were. Nonetheless, the officer said that because it happened on school grounds and a parent was notified and reported it, that he had to ticket us. Except, there was no 'us' to ticket. The kid said that it was the black guy who held the knife and orchestrated everything. Since, I was the only black guy in the group, identification was simple. I was given a ticket to appear in court within 30 days for harassment. If not, a bench warrant would be issued for my arrest. So, there was no getting around telling my mom. I did, and I could sense her disappointment and frustration. Thirty days later, at the arraignment harassment charge was increased to attempted robbery (*though they had no knife, nothing taken was ever taken from anyone, and though no one was physically harmed*). I spent, I believe it was 90 days, (*with 45 days suspended*) in Zebulion Pike. There was never any probation or house arrest options for me. Always detention.

(My grandmother told me once, when I asked what kind of kid was I, was I bad? She said no. Not bad at all, a little mischievous is all. She said that I would put my hands over my ears in church. We laughed at that.)

So, here…I guess, I was a mischievous teenager, no different than any other kid where I'm from. Well, a little uncouth at times, with a particularly dry sense of humor that most people found stale and sarcastic. Yet, you have to understand the environment I grew up in. Colorado is nothing like St. Louis, especially Colorado Springs. See back home in St. Louis by the time I was in sixth grade, and the new kid at Hixon Junior High, it hadn't been there thirty days before I was hit with a Billy-club in the back of the head by my girlfriend as I was getting off the school bus. I was also sprayed with tear gas by a student (not the police) *during a school fight. One day after school, before getting on the bus, my best friend Lendell was hit with brass knuckles by this kid Rodney who'd been trying to instigate a fight with me all week. Rodney was scared of Lendell, but was picking shots with me because he thought his size meant something. He didn't know that I was a scrapper and a self-proclaimed weapon's specialist (I loved Kung Fu movies). I had just gotten a blackjack and I kept my nun-chucks in the inside pocket of my Levi's jean jacket. Rodney hit Lendell and then took off running. Rodney didn't live in our neighborhood, so we didn't catch up to him that day. Anyways, this was a typical school day in ST. Louis and this was considered a good school. And we were considered good kids. I mean you had to be on your toes back home. But I was far from the worst that St. Louis had to offer. The people in Colorado thought I was intense. When in all actuality, in Colorado Springs, I didn't take things seriously enough. And It didn't help that I was a high-energy individual as well as a risk taker. Colorado was boring and particularly slow in comparison to back home. Plus, I rarely saw or met any black people and most of the ones I did meet were white-washed. Which is ironic, because I didn't get hip to selling drugs until I came to Colorado.*

Yet, that wasn't until I met Tony (***who was originally from Houston Texas***) that-that all happened. I was introduced to him by his cousin Tahiesha. She and her little sister also attended Russell Junior High at the time. I had only saw them once or twice during my short stint in school, we hadn't met at the time. But I'd noticed that they walked home in the same direction as I did. One day while walking home from school Tahiesha and her little sister were confronted by a white supremacist stoner. Me and a friend witnessed the taunting from a short distance behind them. We ran up to the girls, the guy and his friend had walked off and were further ahead. I asked the girls what happened. They said that the white male with the long hair had been harassing them all week in and after school, calling them names like blackies, niggers, and monkeys. Much like they were just a minute ago. The girls, trying to avoid them just held their books tight and kept their heads down. When they told me, what happened I was like what! Hell, naw! I yelled from a distance for them fools to stop. They turned around at my voice, seeing it was two black dudes they stopped. So, me and my friend ran up to them; telling them to talk to us like you were talking to them. As soon as the one with the long hair began forming his lips to blurt out a racial slur I popped him square in his mouth and it was on. He got me good in the left ear, causing my ear-ring to split my ear *(my ear is still scarred from that)*. After that, I threw punches till one to the nose downed him. Blood squirted all over his face and my knuckles. I grabbed a fist full of his hair and clocked him two more times before the guys sitting in the parked ambulance chirped the siren and yelled on the bull horn for us to break it up. They were sitting there the whole time just watching. The friend that was with me never got started because the other stoner did not want to fight. He had backed down from the get-go. I didn't care, I was infuriated by them talking that way to the sisters and bullying them. And once, the main dude stepped up to me to own it, I was good with getting my point across to just him at the time. Anyways, it was a few days, maybe more, before I saw Tahiesha and her sister again. I hadn't been at school, but she said no one else bothered them again after that. I wasn't tripping on it one way or the other I was just glad that they felt safe. (In my mind it was no big deal, something I would do again without hesitation whether I knew them or not. We don't play that racial shit back home, it's serious business. And I wasn't about to start letting it fly out here where it seemed even more racial). Tahiesha added that she told her family about what had happened, particularly her cousin Tony. She said that he wanted to meet me and thank me, so she began calling him on her cell phone right then and there. I was like, "for real?" She was like yea, and handed me the phone as he picked up. Tony did, indeed thank me for sticking up for his lil cousins. He said that he lived on the other side of town, but that he was going to come swoop me up later on that night. Crazy as it seemed, he did. He put some money in my hands and began lacing me up on an entirely different level. I spent the next few days with him. Tony took me in from that day forward. I wouldn't be as sharp as I am now, without him. In fact, the very FACT that I am in this predicament is a shame, not only to myself, of course, but also to the level of game given to me by Tony when we were young. *(The street life on any scale is unpredictable and it is not to say that my foot-steps would not have landed me in prison had I stayed in the life. But it damn sure wouldn't have been for something as mindless as petty robbery attached with something as serious as felony murder).* Tony didn't believe in taking those type of risks, deliberately putting oneself in and other's unnecessarily in harms way like stealing and robbery. To him, those were sure ways to get on the police radar. Which was highly counter-productive to any criminal venture let alone, a doe boys' lifestyle. Tony gave me the game; our meeting changed my life. He taught me how to cook crack cocaine, sell it and everything else that came with the dope game. Including being a playa, hustling was everything. Women didn't want you if you didn't have nothing. So, it was 'money over everything.' It was as Big Boi said in the movie 'ATL', "it was grown folks' business." Tony had two cars, a ford tempo and a Park fifth avenue. He was tall and a lot bigger than I was, he looked more like a young twenty-year-old than a teenager. And even though his neutral (*out of the way*) spot was a room in the lower level of his mom's house 'P.T.' also had an apartment of his own. Now, the funny thing about all this, is that Tony and I were the same age. He treated more like his brother than a friend he just met. That meant a lot to me. I looked up to him. He didn't know how much. Tony wasn't a (*feelings*) guy, if you know what I mean. All he knew was that I was from St. Louis and that it was just me, my mom, and my little sister. And that's all, he needed. He didn't know all the details that brought me to Colorado, but he knew that family was just as important to me as it was to him. I was loyal, he needed that…and I needed him. From that day on we were family.

My mother, sister, and I eventually moved from Flintridge to Fountain Colorado. We lived on a street called Alegre circle. To me, it was more like a side street, barely a single car width though two vehicles could pass simultaneously. The area was a mix of low income and middle-class families. My mom commuted from there to Denver to provide for us; sometimes she wouldn't get home till 4 a.m. Despite the fact that we didn't have much my mom never had random men around us. She was independent and didn't believe in having a man around just for financial support. So, when mom went to work those grueling hours I was left to look after my little sister. My sister and I did make friends easily in the neighborhood. There were certain house holds we connected with that shared similar circumstances, which was cool when it came to helping each other out. We we're all struggling to make ends meet. I was a restless teenager, high energy with a hellacious appetite. I was very active. I could eat all day long and never gain a pound. My metabolism was so fast. I always felt like I was starving. Plus, I hated watching mom struggle, working long hours; she was always mentally and physically exhausted. So, I was doing all kinds of things for extra money like helping out at the Loaf-n-Jug that was not even a block away. A brother named Terry was the manager on the night shift. He would let me help stock the freezer and the cooler along with sweeping and mopping the store. In exchange, I could pick a few of my favorite hostess snack, some chips and a pop. Occasionally, he'd fire up a joint with me around closing time. We'd smoke it in the cooler that way we could still look out into the store in case a late customer came in.

When we were done, Terry would let me keep the roach for later, which was usually a half a joint to me. It was a good arrangement. (*I didn't see Tony as much because it was a long way from his stomping grounds which meant a lot more opportunity to get harassed and possibly stopped by the police*). So, he'd rarely risk the drive except for certain occasion. And when he did make the trip to fountain it meant that I'd be staying over-night at his spot anywhere from, a *few days to a few weeks*. Tony didn't do a lot of 'on the block' hustling. Ninety-five percent of his service was on the pager and a cell phone. Which meant that I didn't have as much access to our usual dope spots without him. It also meant that I had to learn my new environment and spread my hustle (*with a pager, a $60-dollar dub, that certainly came sooner than later*). In the meantime, got a job at Wendy's about a half mile up the road. It was my first job with a real paycheck. It wasn't much, but it had its perks like eating a meal of our choice off the menu for lunch. (*The spicy chicken sandwich was my favorite*). In addition to being able to keep all the extra food at the end of the night that would be potentially thrown away. Most of the other employee's had already been working there a while and were burned out which was just great for me, mom, and my little sister. Usually mom had already eaten by the time my shift was over. She really didn't have much of an appetite most days anyway, but my sister and I never got tired of left-over Wendy's. I was happy working, but I couldn't wait to get paid! There was this little antique shop I'd pass on my walk to and from work. I stopped in periodically to convince the owner of my plans. My eyes were set on this glass top dinette table I knew my mom would love. He agreed to hold it for me. It was like eighty-nine dollars. I knew it would make my mom very happy. I loved surprising her with little things when she least expected them. I received my first pay check around Mother's Day! I was good at hiding my feelings so I held my excitement at bay, but I felt so proud when I entered the store with my cashed check that day. Yeah, the whole $164 dollars for two weeks work. My friend Terry helped with the delivery. It was already in the house when my mom came home in place where the old wooden one stood. I told her that it was for Mother's Day even though it was a few days off. I can't remember if we hugged or not, but I do know that she smiled the biggest smile that I'd seen her smile since she left St. Louis. And it was so sad when it had only been a month later that she broke the glass table top. The glass center piece had more sides than a stop-sign and was difficult to find a replacement. She eventually found a company who could replace the glass, but it cost more than the table itself. We couldn't afford it at the moment. However, my mom was determined to restore that table to its original glory when she could. Funny, she ended up keeping the base of that table for another seven years even though I had long since gotten her a new one. Moments like those were precious to me. When I could put a smile on my mother's face and relieve some of the stress from her life. For me, the pressure to contribute to the family was over-whelming. The fast food industry just wasn't enough money for the amount of time it demanded. Between working at Wendy's and going to school things just weren't adding up. It was taking a little more time and a lot more finesse than I expected to see who was doing what in the neighborhood. One day as I was walking home from work my mom spotted me on the side of the road, so she went a little further until she could make the proper U-Turn. She did, then once on my side she pulled off the street into an open lot where I could get in. Before I could get in the car, a K-9-unit police officer pulled in behind my mom with his lights flashing no sirens. He approached as my mother was opening the passenger door for me to get in. With his hand on his weapon, he banged on my mom's window gesturing for her to roll it down. She did, asking him what the problem was? He said that it was illegal to pick up hitchhikers. My mom explained that I was her son and that I was just getting off work. The officer was instinctively angry as if my mother was lying, he told her to step out of the car. Once outside the car, the officer walked my mom over to his patrol car directed her to put her hands on the trunk as he proceeded to frisk her inappropriately, she turned to protest and that's when the officer grabbed my mother aggressively, twisting her arm up her back, she screamed in pain. I quickly jumped out of the car; with one hand holding my mother's arm in that painful position, the other hand grabbing his gun; my mom yelled at me to stop and be still. The officer at the same time ordered me to get back in the car or he would let his dog loose on us. I did as my mom told me and got back in the car; in a quiet rage I wanted to hurt that cop. With me back in the car, the officer let my mom go, wrote her a ticket for whatever, then he got in his patrol car and drove off before us. On the way home, which was a very short drive I remained silent and angry. Once home, my mom didn't want me to go outside right away because I was so angry. My mom's arm was really hurt for a long time after that. I eventually quit my job at Wendy's. It just felt like things were moving too slow for the challenges we were facing at home. I was spending long hours a week at Wendy's and at the end of two weeks it was not even two hundred bucks after taxes. My mind was going a million miles a minute and my metabolism was burning like an inferno. There was never enough food in the house for my highly-active fast developing body. In addition to the pressure I felt to help provide for us, I had to protect my baby sister from the many Fort Carson G.I.'s that were always driving around the neighborhood preying on the little girls and young women. The G.I.'s we're luring girls in with their nice cars and booming systems. The girls didn't know the game, that the government paid for all of it their apartments the cars, everything. And that them fools were basically 'balling on a budget', broke as a joke. They didn't care that my sister was only fourteen years old and she was too young to understand that age mattered. So, I was on guard twenty-four –seven; pulling my sister from the clutches of these horny maggots. I didn't care that these fully-grown men were capable of taking my life if they wanted to. I was prepared to go to whatever lengths I had to in order to protect my baby sister at the time. This caused big fights between my sister and me. She felt that I was somehow robbing her of some grand opportunity to enjoy life on a different level. My sister didn't understand that these men were predators. After countless attempts to detour my sister, even being aggressive and threatening with would be suitors. I felt helpless to provide any real sense of security or advice. The alternative was either I was going to shoot one of them or they were going to be forced to do the same to me. I was an ambitious kid determined to make a difference in our lives. But I couldn't always be there and eventually my sister, thinking she was grown and knew the game, became a victim to the pressures of these men. One in particular, even became accepted by my mom. I personally hated James. He was the nice guy, non-aggressive, a real predator. He worked his way into my mom's heart. I really wanted to do something bad to him. I wasn't fooled by the act. My mom and sister were though. I was angry about it all. But they knew everything, so mentally, I learned to block it all out and chalk it up to it being they way things were in the streets. It was the only alternative to fighting and arguing with my mother and sister or worse. I had enough to be angry about and they didn't seem to share my intuition nor my innate ambition. My nature was different. I was a kid myself, angry and driven to do something more about our living conditions. I hated struggling. I would leave home for days in the streets hustling with Tony. I eventually met another game tight hustler in the neighborhood named Tim. He went by 'Vicious' (may he rest in paradise). He was a Four Corner Hustler. Between him and 'P.T.', I was on. I started smoking weed and drinking. It felt good being able to do things on my own. I felt strong and in control when I was making my own money and my own decisions. I wasn't at a level that would impact my mom and sister on a grand scale yet. But at least, I was able to take some pressure off of them financially by providing for myself and being gone most of the time. My mom didn't like it, but with everything else on her plate she eventually went with it; catching me in between moments to give me an ear full whenever I'd pop up. Whether they knew it or not, my mother and sister were my driving force to succeed in life. I was still in school even though I was in the streets. I was determined to remain educated and make my mark in society. *(It seems that a double life was predestined and somehow weaved into my identity).* From the Colorado Springs viewpoint, I was a threat, a real bad actor. Even though I never started shit or messed with people for no reason. In reality I was just a kid with a lot of heart from a raw city who was heart-broken and home sick about his family situation. The fuel, was that in addition to my problems, I was naturally gifted. I adapted well to pretty much any circumstance. The alternatives weren't always ideal nor the results always positive. But doing something always felt better to me than doing nothing and always complaining Now, here in Colorado getting the street game from real outta town hustlers. I was a quick study and it seemed to fit. However, here I was enrolled at Widefield high and I felt out of place. I talked country and stood out. I was different, too different and for some reason it seemed like I was always getting the short end of the stick in my daily interactions. As the new kid at virtually any school I attended, my unassuming appearance must have given people the impression that I was soft or something. People were always starting shit. I don't know what they thought or were telling themselves, but I always had to prove otherwise. The instigators and would be bullies quickly discovered that what I lacked in physical stature I compensated for with sheer will, tenacity, skill, and aggression. This was crazy because I never started any fights and I was very good at keeping to myself and minding my own business. Yet, I was the one always getting kicked out of school or had the police called on him. I was the bad guy. There was a lot of prejudice and racism in Colorado schools. I couldn't tell if it was because I was black or just different; between the racially motivated squabbles and the fights just because I sounded different and was from out of town. Nevertheless, racism existed in more ways the one. Anyway, my grades in school were good as long as I was there. Eventually, both my grades and progress suffered. The pain of inner world and my ambition were without a healthy filter. It wasn't long before the fights and my intermittent attendance between school and juvenile facilities landed me in alternative classes. There I was in tenth grade at a well-known high school, a fully capable student, in alternative classes. I was balancing the world the only way I knew how. Yet, I was my own family counselor; my own father, my own uncle, my own brother, my own everything. My mom was always on the outside looking in, stubborn in her own world, raising my sister and I trying to make ends meet. In her rants, as she would often do, she encouraged me to make good decisions and always seek higher education and employment of some sort. (*Her rants were her way of talking to you. I'm sure it was challenging for her raising my sister and such an emotionally charged, head strong man-child as much as it was challenging for her and I to connect on a basic level*). My mom and I couldn't talk for five minutes without it becoming an argument. I felt misunderstood so, I didn't talk much about what I was feeling inside with my mom. In the beginning, her motherly instincts kicked in when things weren't quite right with me emotionally, or if I was upset with her and she would do little tender things. Like just take my sister and I for a long drive-stopping at random places; some places were actual places she needed to take care some sort of real business at. Other times, we'd just end up at a park way out somewhere. And sometimes, she'd stop at a park specifically so she could teach us to play tennis. But after a while, I became a professional at masking my emotions. We would go days without talking, sometimes weeks. I was very stubborn in my own way as well. But no matter what I was feeling at some point, I would make it a point to surprise her with simple things like cards, or little gifts to show her that I love her no matter how angry we get at one another. I was like that in general with my mom and sister. I'd buy the little things depending on what holiday or season it was. Then again, there were times when it wouldn't have to be a special day or anything like that. My thoughts were that before I'd buy some female I liked or some girlfriend anything; my mom and sister deserved it first. So, for Valentine's Day, Mother's Day and such, I looked to my home first. We needed the love more. My sister and mom knew that I loved them. I did my best (to show) them. Though they never really seem to fully understand nor comprehend my struggles. At least, that's how I felt. Even with them, I felt alone for some reason. I only felt alive and understood when I was in the streets with 'P.T.' and the guys. We were a small, but well-respected click known for hustling, being strong players, and didn't take shit from no one. Mind you, we were kids and grown men highly respected us. We were in the night clubs and on the scene with many of the heavy hitters at that time in Colorado Springs. Most of the people who were really about something back then, weren't necessarily from Colorado at all. Even our small click, we were all from different cities. P.T. was from Houston Texas, I was from St. Louis Missouri, (dark-skinned) Tank was from New York, Lil Terry was from East St. Louis, Lil Chris was from Cleveland, Ohio, and P.T.'s first cousin Jabbar (rest in paradise) was from Texas also. The south side of Colorado Springs was where it all went down. The clubs etc. The Cloud Nine, The Elks Club, Paradise, Ed's Place. There were other spots like the Bau-Ha Lounge, The La' Jazz, and Bumpers. These were considered the hip-spots where all the black people hung out. The pimps, hoes, players, the pool sharks, dope fiends and doe boys. We were out one evening on Shook's and Run (*I'm sure it's misspelled*) near the school yard one weekend. It was Tony and I, we happened to spot some guys we knew chilling at the park inside the elementary school grounds. School was out of course, they were drinking a 40 ounce. Tony pulled over to holla at them for a minute. A few minutes later, a cop passing by saw the open container. Tabari was twenty-one, so he made him pour the beer out and let them off with a warning for the drinking in public and in a school zone. He began running a routine identification checks on the rest of us. Everyone was code four, yet I was on juvenile probation and I was hot (*I was holding work and a pistol*). When the officer got to me I just took off running. I ran between the grassy area behind some houses dumping the qua (*quarter ounce of crack*) that was in plastic, broken down into bops (*twenty-dollar rocks*), out of my sweat pant pocket. Just my luck, the cop that ran after was nicknamed 'speedy'. I'd actually out ran him initially, up till the point that I slipped on some ice-falling flat on my butt. Boom! He was on me. As he stood me up to my feet, he rummaged through my pockets placing everything on the trunk of the police cruiser that just pulled up. Grabbing all the contents of each pocket in a single handful, out of my right pocket came my pager and two crumpled up $20-dollar bills, and some plastic dangling from his finger-tips. It suddenly dropped to the ground, I stomped at it with my foot trying smash whatever was left in it. The cop snatched me back. It didn't turn to be much, remnants left from my ditching efforts. Once I was cuffed and sitting in the back of the squad car I could see some on looker showing an officer where I threw the gun. I went to the Zeb' pike juvie facility once again. I got my free call. I called P.T. I told him that my bond was $10,000. With a bondsman it would be 15 percent, $1,500. Since it was the weekend I couldn't post bond till that Monday. Well, Monday came. I went to my arraignment. When I got back, I called P.T. to let him know that the simple possession of a controlled 2 substance and weapons charge was increased to 'a special felony' which carried 27 years and my bond was increased to $50,000. I was moved from the juvenile facility to Colorado County Jail 'CJC'. There was nothing he could do for me then. It didn't make sense to put up that kind of money if I was going to have to do some time anyway. I was facing twenty-seven years, 'a special felony' is when they find; collectively, in 'your possession', a gun, drugs, money, and a pager. None of these items were found simultaneously in my possession which was the main prerequisite of 'a special felony'. When the smoke cleared all they really had was some drugs, a little money, a gun, and a pager. I waited it out and soon my juvenile probation officer showed up. His name was Walter Sales *(a big burly guy who reminded me of the actor Jeff Bridges)*. Walt' was a great probation officer. I was being held in (the county jail for adults) in a sectioned off area that housed juveniles who were charged as adults. Walt came to visit me one Friday afternoon. I felt he was always in favor of my progress. It didn't matter that I wasn't perfect; he made me feel as though he cared about my life and what I did with it. So, it was him that recommended me as a candidate for Glenn Mills. Glenn Mills was in Concordville, Pennsylvania. It was the first time the program was ever offered to a Colorado resident. Walt told me about all great the educational programs they had that I could benefit from and explained to me how much a big opportunity it was for me to go. It sounded great to me given the alternative. So, I signed the plea deal. Which was to cop to the weapons and possession of a controlled 2 substance charge. I ended up getting sent out of state with a two-year sentence *(one-year mandatory)*. Which meant that I had to serve a full year before I could be considered for parole. Again, my mom was devastated.

OFF TO GLENN MILLS School for boys.

Glenn Mills was huge! Literally, I was like, "damn, you had to get in trouble to come here, what!" That in itself was insane to me. It was better than any public school I'd ever seen and I 'd be willing to bet that it would rival plenty of the nation's public and private schools for that matter. I felt free, like I had just landed the opportunity of a lifetime. It was very structured. Disciplined. It was run like a boarding slash military school with a hierarchy that you could only climb by positive accomplishment. I knew a lot of kids back home in St. Louis who would love to be at a place like this which was better than our public-school system.

While at Glenn Mills I achieved a lot. It was a good experience sort of like a junior college for juveniles. For example, if you wanted to learn auto mechanics they had a complete auto mechanics shop that could fit ten cars where you worked on vehicles for actual customers outside the compound. Even staff could bring their cars for a discounted price. The vocational building was huge. If you wanted to learn drafting, electronics, and carpentry you built a mini house from the foundation up then you would break it all back down. From academics to sports Glenn Mills had top quality programs. I left Glen Mills with many accomplishments. I got my G.E.D. I received eighteen-month certification in both *retail management* and optometry (*lab tech & dispensing*). I also received team championship trophies for football, indoor & outdoor track, and I won an individual third place power lifting trophy in the 165lb. weight class. I was also received one third of an academic scholarship made in the honor of my then newly assigned Colorado case manager whom had recently passed away. I was eighteen going on nineteen and I felt accomplished. I also managed the first and second floors of the student union at Glenn Mills. I was only months into my two-year sentence when I received a 14-page letter from my mother saying that I had a twin in the form of a female child. I was shocked, in denial, and somewhat upset. I thought, I couldn't possibly have gotten anyone pregnant. I was safe in the streets. Then, boom, it hit me. The only time I had unprotected sex was the night Genita tapped at my bed room window in the middle of the night, on Alegre Circle. Yep. A one hitter-quitter, no rubbers. Yet, what sixteen-year-old would turn down sex from an older woman or any woman for that matter in the middle of the night? Not many, and of course I was no exception. So, there went all my elaborate plans of traveling the world and whatever else was going through my young mind about what I was going to do with my life once I left here and got my stuff together. After doing a year and a half of my two-year, one-year mandatory sentence I was released six months early. I arrived in Denver, Colorado via the old Stapleton Airport. I felt good. I was young and physically fit. So, it was me, mom, my sister Ametrius and her newly born son Teniel lived in a two bed-room apartment in Aurora. It was June 20th, 1994 and I was the new addition to the house hold. I felt good finally being back with my family. A far cry from St. Louis, but for now The River Falls apartment complex in Aurora Colorado was home and it felt good being home. Yet, things were different, very different. Now, I was an eighteen-year-old, father.

Parenting Beyond Tragedy

Chapter 4: **The Sins of The Father**
Young, gifted, and having babies

MISSING PEICES
Time does not discriminate or forgive. Time (itself) is something that a person can never get back from the universe.

As people we miss many things in the course of our lives. We miss appointments, we miss a catch, we miss people, we miss opportunities, and we miss lessons; as parents, we miss moments, precious moments. It's just something that comes along with the territory which is why we invest in all sorts of technology that helps us capture as many exciting moments as possible, especially with our children when they are young. As we get older as parents our memories fade or become cloudy with time, so technology is there to hold the torch for us in timeless fashion.
The only thing that technology can never capture is (time), itself…the actual missed moments.

As a father I have missed out on a lot in the lives of my children. They have missed out on a lot of their father as well. And I have failed tremendously as a father. There are experiences and special moments that can never be recaptured, even in this day and age of technology. The one experience that can never be replaced nor recaptured for me…is the births of all three of my children! I was not present at either of their births (Maraia, Lavie, and Cayline). I have not even seen a video and am not sure if one of those even exist. Talk about a major ball drop in the book of *(once in a life time)* experiences. This was a soul killer. I'm still not sure if I'm over the guilt and shame of it. I've thought about it for years and how that fact alone has affected the intrinsic connection between me and my children. I'm not sure if either of my children even know, but I contemplate the failure. I believe it is the main phenomenon why I'm still struggling to reconnect with my children to this day.

LAVIE
(The First Born)
I came home from Glenn Mills June 20ᵗʰ 1994, exactly one day before Lavie's first birthday. I was as an eighteen-year-old father. My mother lived in Aurora Colorado in a two-bed room apartment. It was me, my younger sister (*Meechie*) Ametrius and my nephew Teniel her newly born son and my mother. It was immediately brought to my attention that Lavie's mother who lived in Colorado Springs was addicted to crack cocaine, so Lavie was with me, my mother and sister eighty-five percent of the time, going back and forth from Colorado Springs and Denver. It was a lot for Lavie. Now, that I was in the picture the mission quickly became to get full custody of my daughter. It wasn't something that Genita, Lavie's mother was opposed to, but it was a work in progress. I still needed to get on track with everything and complete juvenile probation as well. However, there was always open communication between Genita and I. Genita and I were friends prior to conceiving a child together. My mother was the person who helped me get things moving in that direction. My

sister was dealing with a difficult situation with my
nephew; he had birth issues that affected his breathing
and was going thru multiple surgeries at the time. Teniel
was barely eight months old. My sister was only sixteen.
It was heavy for all of us. Yet my sister handled things
well for a baby having a baby. Ametrius was also
instrumental in caring for Lavie as well, doing most of
the baby sitting for me while I went job hunting. I had a
year to do on juvenile parole so getting employed was
my main priority. We lived in walking distance of the
Aurora Mall and many other flourishing businesses in
addition, to the fact that our apartment 'The River Falls'
complex was directly on the bus line of the 15 that
practically took you everywhere. I felt nothing was out of
reach. After several months of diligent searching, I
landed a job at Pager Express. The owner John Cho was
a Korean man with a newly established pager business on
the King Soopers strip mall off of Colfax & Chambers.
He was my boss, my mentor, and more like an older
brother to me. I learned fast, John taught me how to re-
crystal, service, repair, and sale pagers. I got a raise and a
promotion within three weeks. I was assistant manager. I
had my own desk, business cards and helping close the
store on most day's things couldn't have been better. I
was also enrolled part-time at The Community College of
Aurora for general studies and psychology 101. I wasn't
absolutely sure of what I wanted to pursue at the time. I
was making good money and felt good about being able
to provide for myself and my daughter as well as help out
at home. After about six months into work a martial arts
studio opened up just doors down on the same strip as my
job. I was elated; I've always wanted to train martial arts

since I was a kid. I met the owner and instructor Tommy Johnson. I was surprised to see that he was black, a native of the Montebello neighborhood, and that he was a (three-time world champion)! Tommy was about 5'11 not quite six feet and weighed about a hundred and sixty or seventy pounds! His accomplishments were highly impressive to say the least. I of course, asked every question as to his skill level in comparison to Bruce Lee of whose life I had extensive knowledge of. Tommy's skill was extraordinary. I signed up and began training immediately. My schedule was (*work, school, training*); parenting… (*Spending time with Lavie*) Well, this was very difficult. On her days off, my mom was at home with the grand children along with my sister. I was ambitious and wasn't home much. I paid my sister for baby sitting though it wasn't necessarily a contract between us I understood that she had to receive some type of benefit for her time. Neither mom or my sister expected payment as a prerequisite for babysitting. We just didn't view the situation like that. Meechie had a son and I had a daughter. We all contributed to our family situation which was to make it work by the best means necessary. When it came time for me to take Lavie with me she never wanted to go she would always throw a tantrum and I mean it was quite a spectacle! She did not want to go with daddy. Lavie was so accustomed to being with her grandmother and her aunt. I was a stranger. I never said anything to my mom or sister but it broke my heart. It was difficult for us to bond. I just blocked it all out. I felt that as long as my daughter was provided for that I was at least doing my part for now. Though Lavie was with us eighty percent of the time, she was still going back and forth to the springs to stay with her mom and her other siblings. Everything must have been just a blur with Lavie as far as how she looked at me. She knew I was her father but it was awkward for us. I had so much going on as an eighteen-year-old father. I was always on the move. My life was one big hustle, working, training, and school, being a parent and trying to enjoy youthful activities; In addition to being a young father. Things got a little overwhelming. I eventually, dropped the Aurora Community College thing. My passion was martial arts and I saw a bright future in it even though I was a beginner. Still, things were working out well at the time. I loved my life and it felt as if I were finally being productive and making my mark as a young man.

Lavie's mother Genita and I were discussing me having full custody of our daughter. Lavie was with me and my mother and sister eighty-five percent of the time now any way, especially since her mother was struggling with drug addiction. Lavie was 5 years old at the time, was briefly in my custody; when I allowed her aunt Ametrius to take her to visit her mother and siblings in Colorado Springs. My sister was supposed to bring her back to Denver with her; instead my sister took the liberty to leave her with her mother and siblings for the weekend. During that time, there was an incident at the home. The police were called; Lavie was among the several children taken from the home and placed in social services care. When the dust cleared I was contacted immediately. I was informed that I was labeled as a neglectful parent and in order to prove otherwise and get full custody of my daughter it would be a process. That process included proving that I could provide a safe and stable living environment as well as provide for her over-all wellbeing. Tasha and I had recently settled into our new apartment and weren't in it long before we learned of the death of her beloved sister which shortly after, the emotional trauma proved to be too much for our relationship; we were in crisis, separated and that put me in a desperate situation between me and Tasha's old apartment and my mom's apartment. I wasn't in the best position to get Lavie back, at the moment. It was going to take some time to get things back in order. In the meantime, I was required to have observed-evaluated visits with Lavie in Colorado Springs; I lived in Denver. I was travelling back and forth, trying to get my own place, struggling to make the appointments on time, it was difficult. The break-up with Tasha left an unfulfilled lease agreement left my credit in question. So, it was next to impossible to find a place in a decent environment in time for a social service inspection. That moment came upon me pretty quick. And I didn't want to inform them about the issue. It would only them more reason to delay the process of getting Lavie back. And solidify their allegations that I wasn't capable of taking care of my daughter. Lavie couldn't afford any more delays. The entire ordeal was already traumatizing enough for Lavie. (*Especially, when it came time for me to leave during those scheduled visits. She was so confused, and hurt thinking that I was never going to return*). No, I could not risk that look in her eyes again. I was out of options. My mom had to take over as legal guardian. My mother's home was one that my daughter knew and trusted. Plus, it was the only option we had in order to keep Lavie from getting stuck in the system. Nevertheless, the delay was inevitable. *(Just the thought of my five-year-old child alone in a dim lit room. In some strange building, surrounded by strangers; crying, begging to go home and being told no, was killing me)*. I literally, wanted to just walk in there and walk out with my baby. The energy of that place, that house was simply just that-dim. My baby must be terrified I thought. I was angry. My spirit was unsettled in the worst way. Still, in order for Lavie to go home with her grandmother meant paperwork, paperwork, paperwork.

THE BIRTH OF CAYLINE
(The Second Light)
When Amanda and I met; I was still working at Pager Express. We were introduced to one another by a mutual acquaintance named Eric. Eric was a hustler and aspiring business man. He initially described Amanda to me as a cool white girl that was into black men. He said that he thought Amanda and I would be a good fit because she was ambitious and independent. Bottom line, she was a hustler. He said that he would introduce us; I really didn't believe him at first or even thought that he would follow thru. Besides lying a lot, Eric was a salesman and was always pitching his next big business deal. So, I only believed half of what he ever told me.

Eric brought Amanda to my job a couple days later. She was cute and very stylish. She was about 5'4; she wore a Nike nylon sweat suit. Her hair was in a ponytail tucked through a matching Nike hat, an inch width gold herringbone necklace lay just across the top of her breast. We shared a quick introduction, exchanged phone numbers and I told her that I got off at six p.m. we could hook up then to discuss our plans. Though I worked full time at the pager store I sold crack cocaine on the side. It was sort of prearranged by Eric that we were hooking up as business partners and that anything more would be on us. Amanda was in between jobs at the time, but had some money saved up. She was accustomed to selling weed with Eric but she felt that the money was too slow. Eric of course, had gave her an update on me and my get down, so she agreed that it might be a good idea for us to team up. I told Eric to set up the meeting. She agreed to meet me, I got off at 4 p.m. I wanted to make sure that Amanda and I were on the same page before when did any business together. Later that evening, Amanda and I hit it off pretty well. We were both in agreement that our arrangement was strictly just business. I could tell that she was attracted to me on a personal level. Amanda was cute, but I put it in my mind that I wasn't going to get involved on that level; back then, business was my idea of friends with benefits. Though we made a good team and some good money together, my plan was to keep it there. It also, meant that we spent a lot time together. Yet, as with most good things and good friends *(time)* will only increase the bond one way or the other. Amanda and I did become closer, but she became more attached to me than I allowed myself to be with her. I was attracted to her; she was very smart, intuitive, and affectionate with a great since of humor. But I suppressed my feelings for her, the money was more important to me than a serious relationship. We both loved the money. She was getting what she wanted and so was I; a fair exchange isn't robbery as the saying goes. Our relationship was only bumpy when Amanda wanted more of my time, emotion, and affection than I was willing to give. Not that it was a completely bad thing, it wasn't. I just wasn't willing to be committed to anyone. I was almost nineteen with a child already and entirely different idea's of where I wanted my life to go. I was stacking my bread, preparing for a complete exodus out of my mom's apartment. But, being involved with Amanda had its perks. It meant that I wouldn't have to pay for motels all the time, trying to flex my independent muscles when I wasn't staying at my mom's place. Which I did a lot when I didn't have Lavie.

Amanda had a very nice apartment. Both times we had sex was at her place, we used protection the first time. Honestly, I really didn't want to get intimate with her. But she was putting in a whole lot more than what was initially expected and agreed upon. *(And I wanted to continue receiving the added benefits. So, I had to give a little to continue getting a lot more).* Yet, that night, the sex was unmemorable for both of us. It was terrible. I was holding back in every way, preventing any real connection other than our sexual organs doing what they were designed to do. This was different for me because I usually take pride in my ability to please and go all out, but not that night. I just wasn't into it and Amanda intuited my disinterest immediately. She was more hurt about my unwillingness to open up and let go with her than she was disappointed about the performance. The (disconnect) was obvious. Still, she didn't give up her efforts to win me over. The second time, I could have sworn she planned it and timed it to the 'T'. I was in the shower at her apartment. Amanda was supposed to be at work, yet she popped up right as I was literally still soaping up. I had a key and I called her prior to my arriving at her place to inform her that I would be there to get fresh and get back to the spot. Low and behold, surprise! There she was coming in from her lunch break to hop in the shower with me (unprotected sex) a one hitter-quitter, the inception of Cayline though at the time, I had no idea. When I finally got the news that she was in fact pregnant I was at work at Pager Express. Amanda called me unexpectedly; I took the call at my desk saying that she was three or four months pregnant. I was shocked and a little upset. I was shocked by the fact we only had unprotected sex once. I was upset because Amanda had said that though she had been trying to get pregnant by a black man for years; she had recently found out (with her last boyfriend) that medically it had become physically impossible. It was something about her uterus being upside down...or something like that. I don't remember now, exactly. But it was real enough for her to even share the condition with my mom. She even had medical papers to prove it. Nevertheless, those facts weren't the reason I let me guard down in the shower that day. It simply was, what it was. I was in the shower. Yet, here in this moment on the phone at work the thought that she set me up did cross my mind as I responded to her, "I thought you couldn't get pregnant?" She replied in obvious surprise and amazement that it was in fact unbelievable. Still, I said, "you're getting an abortion right." Amanda said that she was too far along. The rest of the conversation is too ugly for me to recant for Cayline's sake nor to have Amanda re-live through the words of this book. However, I will say that I was the most horrible person I can ever recall being to any woman in my life; to Amanda that day.

Ironically, the day Cayline was born I was at work again. I did not get to witness my daughter's birth. I did however get to see her in the incubator and I fell in love with her from that moment on. She was so beautiful and peaceful. That was also the moment that if Amanda was lying about her medical status before or whatever concerning her initial inability to give birth, I forgave her. I told myself that I would not bring it up to her ever again. (*It didn't mean that <u>she</u> **forgave** <u>me</u> for the venomous things I said to her in my office over the phone that day*). Nevertheless, despite my ignorance, cruel words and personal indifference to the situation *(with having another child out of wedlock)*; as parents we decided that we both had to do some things differently. We were friends, but we weren't a couple, and that meant that she was going her way and I was going mine. While we both agreed to provide for Cayline. A lot had indeed changed between Amanda and I since the pregnancy and birth of our daughter. No longer involved in the street life, Amanda felt that she would need some extra support being a mom and getting on her feet in the right way. She moved back with her mother and step-dad in Evergreen Colorado. In addition to being far removed from the enchanting thoughts of her and I being together; infused with the responsibility of being a new mother, Amanda became controlling and possessive within our co-parenting dynamic. Whereas we'd agreed on equal parenting time when it was my turn to spend time with our daughter she didn't want that time to be independent of her presence. I couldn't take my daughter with me without a conflict. I eventually paid five hundred dollars retainer fee for a lawyer and one hearing where we established documented equal parenting rights. Still, the arrangements were not ideal to me or the court order. Cayline's grandmother highly disapproved of me being her father. So, I wasn't allowed to pick Cayline up from where they all stayed. I had to meet Amanda at some strip mall slash galleria called 'The Tower Plaza' I believe it was. Our father and daughter time were spent walking around this little mall with Cayline in a stroller and her binky, wow… Yes, this was the form of quality time for Cayline and I for these scheduled (every other week) visits. I tolerated it for the time being, mainly because I felt guilty of how I treated Amanda during our business arrangement and personal interactions. (*No, I never laid a hand on Amanda. I wasn't that guy and we were never officially boyfriend and girlfriend*). However, I fully internalized the role of it is "just business" on every level. It was intense at times, especially whenever Amanda tried to connect with me on an emotional level. I was shrewd and indifferent; a complete 360 compared to who I truly was on a regular basis. And rightfully so, Amanda felt that she never experienced an ounce of my tenderness or compassion toward her as a human being. Which was more an emotional-mental exaggeration on her part, than absolute truth. I am naturally a warm and caring person. But, it was 90% business, and 10% personal. And I made sure that she was reminded of it every step of the way; after all, we were both in agreement when we started this thing of ours. Deep down, it did bother me. Because like I said, *"I am naturally a compassionate person and generally go out of my way to show that side of myself to people, especially those I'm close to."* Again, the *benefits* of our agreement outweighed any inner conflict and my better judgement on my part. Ethically, she may have deserved much more of who I was as a young man back then. Yet, principally, I learned very early on that there was no room for emotions and feelings in the street game. You got to WIN. That meant taking as few losses as humanly possible and definitely not taking (any) *foreseen-unnecessary* ones. So, I embodied the shrewd business role deeply, so much that it may have created lasting emotional wounds for both of us. Amanda and I had agreed upon equal co-parenting time with our daughter. But like I said, the arrangements for my father-daughter time were ridiculous. Yet, somehow, I felt guilty for my initial reaction to the pregnancy and all. So, I endured the current parenting arrangements for the time being. The time spent with Cayline made up for the bullshit arrangement. The Plaza was small. And our time consisted of me and strolling my baby *(who hadn't quite learned her first words yet)* around this plaza having imaginary conversations. We did laps, passing by her mom who sat on a bench as she observed me in this pretend space with my baby. I would stop periodically, to sit and talk with Amanda. This was our daddy daughter time. Why couldn't I take my child with me like any other normal parent in a co-parenting situation? Why was that so difficult for Amanda? After all, we were actually there in (that space) because I had retained a lawyer. Who got the judge to see to it that I did indeed get my equal parenting time. Yet, here I was still, enduring unrealistic terms and conditions outside of the courts' ruling…why? Because **I felt guilty**. I was being more sensitive to her emotional needs and petty mind games than I was my own logical expectations and legal rights to spend time with my child. Rights, that I literally spent money and fought for. Crazy, right. Yet, here I was, (*for the time being*) in temporary adherence to Amanda's terms. Anyways, **during what would become my last father-daughter meeting at the plaza**, Amanda was expressing to me that she was planning to explore some employment options in California and that Cayline would be staying with her grandmother (Amanda's mother) instead of with me. She said that her mother would continue our visiting arrangement. I was upset and objected to the that part of the plan. Again, (guilt) and the unspoken fact that (I) still had one foot in the streets kept me from pressing the gas on the issue and creating more conflict. Amanda said that she would only be gone for about two to three months. I believed and trusted in her ambition and financial resolve; not to mention her new drive of being a mother. Reluctant, yet, understanding to the fact that we were now co-parents, I agreed. I trusted the process even though I knew how Amanda's mother felt about me and the fact that she had a baby by a black man. Nevertheless, next my visit with Cayline scheduled through her grandmother went as planned. We met at the same place as before and Cayline and I had our father-daughter time in the little plaza, galleria/mall etc. The next time the moment arrived for our regularly scheduled visit…I called, no answer. I called again no answer. A week passed, I called, and the phone number was disconnected. I called again to make sure I'd dialed the right number… same thing, the recording sounded off, "I'm sorry the number you have just dialed is no longer

in service please check the number and try your call again." Beeeeep, that was it.
(Pre-internet) I was lost....

As far as I knew Cayline was with her grandmother and I had no idea where they were. Amanda and her mother went to great lengths for me not to have any contact with them. I was distraught and in search of them four years prior to the day I entered the Colorado Department of Corrections.
Maraia
(The youngest, The Gemini)
Born during the storm of Love.

It was a normal business day at work; customers were in and out of the pager store. John, my boss was at the register. I was coming in from lunch with my meal in hand when I stumbled thru the door staring at one of the browsing customers. Startled she turned around smiling, we simultaneously said, "Hi." I put my food on my desk and asked if I could help. She said she needed to pay her monthly bill. After that she purchased some pager accessories; as I rung her items up I introduced myself and asked her name and phone number. Tasha was a light-skinned Serena Williams in jeans. I would describe how fine she was but that athletic backside of hers which caused me to stumble is all I can remember that day! The day Tasha and I first met. How was I to know that-that stumble would be the symbol of things to come...Tasha was eighteen, I was twenty. We stumbled along in love ever since.

Things moved fairly quickly between me and Tasha. She lived in Green Valley Ranch with her parents Mr. & Mrs. Vermont, her older sister Latonya (May she forever be blessed in peace), and her younger sister Daniel. They were a part of the 1ˢᵗ Christian Assembly Baptist Church led by pastor Tombs. Tasha's family was very big, close knit, loving and supportive. Tasha also had a seven-month-old son named Nalajaun. I didn't know much about Nathan, Najee's father except that he was a stable young man. I asked Tasha about their relationship with their son. It was important to me to know what the situation was surrounding that dynamic so I would understand how to best fulfill my role in Nalajaun's life while in complete support of the relationship with him and his father. Tasha and I were getting pretty attached to one another. Her so was quite the inspirational bundle of joy. I insisted that Najee call me Dee not Daddy. I wanted to ensure that I nurtured a strong bond of love and care along with the distinction that I am not his father. That title is something special that only Nalajaun and his father should share because it can never be replaced or substituted. Tasha was several months away from prom and graduation. We decided not to have sex until then. Tasha was a little sheltered compared to my St. Louis upbringing. In my eyes, she was everything that I was missing in my life. Tasha represented love, structure, a strong connection with her family, stability, and a healthier future. And that was something I was fully willing to give to, nourish, and protect with all my power. I hadn't been inside a church nor had I even considered a church home since I left St. Louis. My grandmother's church, Jesus Christ Nazarene Baptist

Church was the only church home I knew since I was a kid. Tasha had convinced me to come to her family's church. Everyone knew we were moving too fast, so when we started talking about moving in together and getting married they all warned us to slow down. Tasha's mom, Mrs. Vermont sat us down and spoke with us about what would be expected of us as a couple, as young parents, and what it all meant being husband and wife. She even suggested youth marriage counseling with the church. Overall, Mrs. Vermont (*God rest her beautiful soul*) told us to take it slow. We didn't.

I proposed to Tasha one night in the one-bedroom apartment that I shared with a partner of mine named Tank. Tank and I went way back since the time I lived in Colorado Springs. Tank was one of the reasons we were able to level-up back in the day. He, Humphrey aka 'Hump', and P.T. were getting work from New York to bring it back to Colorado. A long, long story-short. Some things went down and now Tank was in Denver on federal parole, he just served five years. So, he was adamant about staying off the radar, he was working a square job at Foot Locker at the Aurora Mall. It was just a front till he got back on his feet. Tank always had a plan brewing, he wouldn't be down for long-at-all. In the meanwhile, I was still on, so I turned over all of the connects and clientele that I had, to Tank. Not that Tank needed help hustling, no, Denver was just new territory for him. Which made perfect sense to me at the time. My heart wasn't in anymore. At least, not in that avenue. *Innately, I will always be a hustler. But in my heart, I believed I had what it took to make an impact on the other side of the scale).* Besides, there was no way I was going to have a life with Tasha without having both feet on the same side of the tracks. So, just like a square, I jumped. A sucker in love.

Anyways, Tasha said yes to my proposal. We were moving faster than a speeding bullet. A month or so later we moved into our first apartment. It was a two bedroom on ground level. I furnished the entire living room and kitchen, including a complete entertainment sound system courtesy of Rent-A-Center. There were a few guys there that owed me some favors. Tasha kept her Queen Size bed and bedroom set she had at her mom's house. So, our place was pretty nice, it had a peaceful aura. Except for one thing, neither of us knew how to grocery shop the right way. She was accustomed to living a sheltered life at home with her family and I was accustomed to the fast life, street life, everything was on the go (*like a college kid minus the college campus*). So, we never had a properly stocked refrigerator. It was crazy! Well, we did have money which meant we ate out ninety percent of the time. Which didn't matter to Tasha. As far as she was concerned, we never had any food, damn the money. We were so bad at grocery shopping that I gave Tasha several hundred dollars to go grocery shopping on the account she grabbed her aunt Rene (her uncle Jodi's wife) and her big sister Latonya to go along with her. She had spoken with them over the phone before coming so they brought some of the frozen meats Tasha's mom's house. When they got there, they couldn't believe how bare our situation was. Of course, Tonya cracked some jokes about it. She was funny like that. We all had a good laugh about it. When they got back several hours later our fridge heavily stocked. It was a great. For the first time our place felt like a completely accessorized home! Life was good then. Tasha and I were young in love, young parents, trying to figure it all out as we went along. Time seemed to fly by. I was well into my martial arts training and wining tournaments. Tasha and her closest friends were always laughing and cracking jokes about me and my karate classes. Surprisingly Tasha was also very supportive of my martial arts ambitions. Ironically, Tasha and her thirteenth month old son Najie were the 'only familiar' faces at all of my tournaments. It seems that's all I needed because I always brought home first place. (*Shout out to my Sifu 'Tommy Johnson' Three- time world champion, a Montebello native and owner of The Institute of Fighting Arts Dojo in Aurora*). Needless to say, things were going well in Tasha's and I first apartment. We were like jackrabbits, she was my Viagra and I was her addiction. All was well, then, boom! In came the storm; **A Hell Storm.**

The phone rings… It's very early in the morning (*Tasha answers it*) "hello" (*a long pause*) … (*then*) What? What! No! No! She drops the phone collapsing to the floor. She's crying and screaming frantically. What's wrong? What happened! Tasha baby, what- Tonya's dead! They killed my sister! Tonya's dead…she groaned in agony as if the sun fell from the sky taking her soul with it. Tasha's screams sent an eerie chill throughout my body. She was inconsolable, her world was shrouded in darkness and I was just a shadow within the void of her despair. I picked up the phone. I don't remember who was on the other end; her mom, Uncle

Jodi, Mr. Vermont…I'm not sure now but the instructions, directions rather to meet the rest of the family at the crime scene. It was at pastor Tombs' residence in Montebello, where Latonya breathed her last vital breath on this earth. She was brutally taken from us while home sitting fifteen-year-old Jennifer Tombs.

When Tasha and I arrived at the scene, everyone was in heart wrenching agony. The men were hurt and infuriated. We wanted to do something to whoever was responsible. We had heard that there were males present, a party, no one knew the whole story. It seemed like a life time had passed before Tonya's body was brought out. Then there she was. We were all standing together when Tasha collapsed in several family members' arms in a fireball of pain. As Tonya's body was loaded into the ambulance it felt like a slow-motion picture. For what seemed like an eternity, yet lasted only fractions of a second. *It was the eye of the storm.* Tasha went ballistic. She didn't see me though I was a breaths' length away from her the entire time. She couldn't feel my soul wrapping around her trying to console her. I was invisible. Tasha was shuffled out of my arms and into a close relative's vehicle as if I was not there at all. I never saw the Tasha (*I knew and loved*) ever again…she was never the same.

At the funeral service, I was among the pallbearers along with Tasha's father Mr. Vermont, her brothers Mark and Herman, Uncle Jodi, and Cousin Casey. It was a lovely honor. (*Tonya was a great artist and I loved LaTonya like a sister; she was a truly graceful and inspirational person to be around. Tonya often called me "Bruce Dee" and I called her Monica after the singer because she looked like a light skinned version of the star, plus they had the same hairstyle. It was our way of bonding. I miss her dearly.)*

Tasha and I still lived together. However, the energy inside our apartment was like the twilight zone. There was a wall around her heart and soul…there was Tasha, and then there was Tasha's heart. I no longer held the key; her emotions were like the tides of the ocean and I was the seaman without a ship or a GPS navigations system.

Our relationship took a drastic turn. There were long instances of silence. Our apartment nor our hearts was any longer a space where we connected and communicated with one another. We began to argue a lot, then one night we had a huge fight. We broke up. Several of Tasha's male family members came over to our place that same night; she went to live back with her mom, dad, and little sister Daniel in Green Valley Ranch. Some months went by; our apartment still had about six months left on the lease. It was difficult for me but I stayed there on and off while Tasha and I argued over phones calls and voicemail messages about what was what, and whose was whose. We had officially gone our separate ways. It was a little over three months when I heard she was back with her ex, Nalajaun's father. The reunion was short lived. The rumor was that Tasha was pregnant. Something I didn't know at the time when we broke up. I had moved on as well, just a rebound at best when Tasha finally told me about the pregnancy. Tasha and I agreed upon getting an abortion. Before we made the final decision, Tasha and I met up at the King Soopers strip mall parked between Turbo Tax & 707 I asked if this is what she really wanted to do; to get the abortion and truly go our separate ways. I was involved with a woman named Nicole at the time. I wanted to be sure about Tasha before I put my all into moving forward. (*Nicole and I recently met through our children Nicole lived in the same apartment complex as my mother. Nicole and I weren't too serious, but we connected with one another from the very beginning and I cared for her, yet she was fully aware of the situation and knew that I still loved Tasha.*) So, the day Tasha and I discussed everything as we sat in the car, leaving no stone unturned, at the end I asked if this is what **she truly wanted to do… she said yes**. She felt that this would be the best decision, that we get the abortion and do our own thing. I asked again to make sure…because I was looking her to say no and that she wanted to make things work. Again, she affirmed her position; we ended our conversation very civil and respectable.

On the scheduled abortion day, we went to the clinic together; I paid for eighty-five percent of the fee she said that her insurance would take care of the rest. I asked if she wanted me to go in with her, she preferred that I waited in the car. When she came out some hours later I asked how she felt, she said that the abortion was final and that she was okay. I could tell that she wasn't, but she insisted that she was cool. The ride back was silent. I dropped her off at her mom's in Green Valley Ranch; from there we went our separate ways. The months flew by and then…boom. An **ATOMIC BOMB.**

Six months had passed. Nicole, her children and I are bonding and getting along great when one night I received a page. I called back from Nicole's apartment. Tasha tells me that she is having a baby, our baby. I'm blown away. I'm very angry, asking a lot of questions along with some allegations as well. I'm like shit, it ain't mine. I heard about you going back to your baby daddy. She admitted that she did, but the times didn't add up. We both did the math then I asked to speak with her mom, Mrs. Vermont. Mrs. Vermont confirmed the pregnancy and was persuading me to come be with Tasha and the baby at their house, saying that I could have Latonya's room. I express my dismay with all this, Tasha's dishonesty the whole nine, including my current situation. I adored Mrs. Vermont and respected her insight and the fact that she just lost a daughter weighed heavily on my heart. I felt trapped. I loved Nicole; we had all of our cards on the table from jump. We were two peas in a pod, as they say. Nicole was two years older than me, California raised and real down to earth, we had a lot in common. She was also a great example of a single mother who was a well-balanced co-parent with the fathers of her children. They had healthy connection and communication with one another. I began breaking down the entire situation to Nicole about Tasha, the pregnancy, and the live-in situation. Nicole lost it! She knew full and well that a man could take care of his children without being there with the mother of his children; Hell, she was living proof! The idea of me going to back to Tasha on the account of the baby, she wasn't having it! I felt pulled in both directions, from Nicole's point of view things were pretty cut and dry (rightfully so). Yet, for me, the weight of it all was a lot heavier than Tasha's deceit and betrayal. It was also, sad to say, heavier than the love and connection I had with Nicole and her lovely children, Asia and Shaquan. My lack of wisdom, maturity, doubled with inner guilt, delusion and disappointment; ran much deeper. (*It ran all the way back to my broken home and the day I found out that I was having my first child Lavie and I wasn't with the mother of my child. I felt like I failed again with Cayline, my second child out of wedlock.*) I certainly didn't believe that a marriage or being with someone because we shared a child together equaled a perfect home. Or a 'happy' one for that matter. But I was chasing a fairytale romance in a field of **mistakes** and **dreams**. As self-serving and self-righteous as it sounds… I was chasing my failures…Somehow, I felt that the knowledge and experience of my past would prevent me from making all the wrong decisions in life when it came to having kids of my own and building a safe and secure future for them. After all, I understood firsthand what a broken home and a scattered family unit does to a child. In the midst of all the drama I weighed the options. At the crossroads of my own doing. I had a decision to make. Tasha was due any time.

Ultimately, I made the decision to go be with Tasha in Green Valley Ranch. On the outside, *in this self-righteous world in my mind,* I felt as if I made the hard but morally sound decision. Mentally and emotionally, I was lost in the sauce. My inner turmoil weighed me down on so many levels. *At the time of Latonya's passing, I made a promise over her grave that no matter what happened between her sister and I, that I will always be there for Tasha; a mere delusion at best.* I was carrying this self-imposed burden with me like sap in a Missouri Maple sap tree. No matter what Tasha dished out, *with the exception of being unfaithful if it was forgivable*; because of that vow, that promise, I eventually found a way to forgive her. All the while, telling myself that she had suffered the most. Losing her sister. She was young. She nor I knew how to navigate those feelings. So, I'll bare the burdens of her emotional mistakes. In reality, I was just Tasha's emotional door mat. I was living in this self-righteous extreme inside my head trying to save my little world at the expense of Nicole's broken heart and the bond we shared. (*I was chasing a ghost*). Nicole was crushed. When everything settled. Nicole and I remained friends. There was no reason not to. She hadn't done anything wrong. I made that part very clear to Tasha upon our reunion. And I upheld the integrity of that friendship without ever betraying the relationship between Tasha and I. There were even times I was there for Nicole through some tough situations that were very-heavy emotionally and somewhat, financially. But no matter how heavy the circumstances were; Nicole never shed another tear around me. Nicole was no longer open nor vulnerable with me beyond our friendship. She was adamant about making sure I stood on my choice. Though I am an 'old soul' in that aspect and didn't need any help standing on my decision. I respected her resolve. She never wavered nor attempted to seduced me back from Tasha.

Finally, the day came for Tasha to give birth. She was at the hospital surrounded by family. I was somewhere in

Aurora making runs and smoking blunts with my partner Patrick when I got the call. It was Tasha's aunt Rene going off! "Dee, get your butt down here to the hospital ASAP! Tasha's in labor about to have the baby at any moment." So, I asked Patrick if he wanted to roll with me to see the birth of my child, he said yes, but he had to be back in time for curfew; he was on ankle monitor probation. Patrick had about an hour and a half, we took the gamble. Night time traffic was heavy; the drive took longer than expected. We arrived at the hospital reeking of marijuana smoke and were met equally with stares of disappointment from medical staff and all of Tasha's family members. Patrick and I went to the designated family waiting room. Then I was quickly ushered off to wash my face and hands before I was taken to the room where Tasha was in labor, hooked up with the epidural, we had light conversation between breaths; forty-five minutes or so had passed and Patrick had to be back soon, very soon. We were in Denver; He lived in Aurora and with the traffic it would take another forty minutes there and back. I explained the dilemma to the family, no one else was gonna leave and take Patrick anywhere. If 'P' didn't make it back in time he would possibly be arrested the next day, he'd already had some conflict with his probation officer as it was. So, against everyone's advice and better judgment, I took him. No sooner than Patrick and I were on the highway, maybe ten to fifteen minutes into the drive my phone rings...The tone was flat, "Dee, she had the baby, it's a girl she named her Maraia Lynnmnik Davis." I could feel the energy through the phone, there was so much disappointment in the voice on the other end.

That event marked the moment I became a three-time loser. I had missed the birth of all my children (three strikes) I'm out. **#Sins of The Father**

Parenting Beyond Tragedy

<u>Chapter 5</u>: **The Sins of the mother**
I imagine that it is a terrifying experience for the mother of a child whose father goes to prison, equally, if not even more terrifying for the child. For the mothers of my children I can't begin to tell you what they were going through when they discovered that I was in prison. There must have been an avalanche of emotions, an earth quake of feelings, and some chemical reactions that they probably couldn't even describe let alone, process. I cannot pretend to know what that's like from a mother's perspective. After all, what parent prepares for something like this?

I have *three different baby mommas*. However, I am going to share with you the 'Sins of the Mother' from my perspective as it relates to the mothers of my children and the relationship experience we shared. Though all of my children are affected by my absence, one no less than the other. I am starting with the experience that was most alarming for me as an incarcerated (*absentee*) father, as much as it was damaging by way of (*non-action*) on the part of my child's mother. #Subtle toxicity. I'm talking about the relationship I shared with Tasha. The mother of my youngest daughter Maraia. Tasha was the only woman out of the three that I was actually in a committed relationship with. Her and I had been through a lot together. I thought that those experiences, at the very least, would have held heavy merit in moments like this; (i.e. my incarceration). We share a child regardless of the unfortunate nature of the situation. Tasha and I were even engaged at one point. I was even a pallbearer at her sister's funeral. It was with Tasha that I felt I would have shared a deeper bond and a healthier level of communication with at such a pivotal moment in our lives. So, the lack thereof during this ordeal, was shocking to me. None of it mattered. Wow, I thought. And you would have to know more about our history to know just 'How' shocked I truly was. But, despite Tasha's silent, (*ignore it and it will go away*) approach to the matter. I continued with my best efforts to keep the channel of communication open throughout the years for the sake of our daughter. However, my humble efforts proved fruitless.

In 1999, the gravity of the situation was evident. Besides an acquittal, the best possible out-come of my trial would still mean that my children would be without their father for a very long time. So of course, I expected Tasha to live out her best life regardless of my fate, which indeed she did. In fact, when I found out from Lisa, a mutual friend, that Tasha was five months pregnant and about to be married. I very candidly said to Tasha, over a phone call, that it didn't matter to me who she was married to. That I would put her and her husband on my visitor's list if they'd just bring my daughter to see me whenever possible. I extended the olive branch and invitation. I did my best to invoke the spirit of co-parenting beyond the tragedy of all this mess. I expressed how important it was that we maintain some type of communication for our daughter's sake. And what little connection we are able to maintain over the years would be vital to Maraia as she grows up and has to process this situation. I deeply apologized to Tasha for failing them. I actually spent the better part of the first decade, apologizing over and over and over and over. I poured my out my soul in more ways than one could imagine. But nothing got through. My level of accountability, self-responsibility, love, compassion, self-respect, guilt, shame, whatever. You name it. It was never matched. It was never considered. Hell, it didn't matter. *(I) didn't matter*. And apparently, Tasha felt It wouldn't matter to Maraia either once she became of age. Because I never received a visit from my daughter at any stage of the process. In fact, I never received a reply to the countless gifts nor letters I'd written to my baby. Tasha never even answered the phone after our last conversation despite placating the entire idea of us co-parenting through this difficult situation; her response… was almost two decades of silence.

A silence, that was only temporarily broken by (my efforts) in the form of a brief phone call that had finally gotten through after all these years. Maraia was sixteen and a half in 2014.
"What you do speaks so loudly that I cannot hear what you say." –Ralph W. Emerson
Over the years, in agony, I continued to write and send pictures of myself, personal drawings, and gifts through Angel Tree and other prison outreach services. There was never any acknowledgement or communication that indicated that Maraia was receiving any of the letters and gifts. I never received any pictures of Maraia of how she was doing. I was in limbo for years. It was torture. As it was, my fate was sealed. I was sentenced to life in prison and my greatest fear was that I didn't want them to ever feel that I abandoned them, didn't love or want them, nor that any of this was their fault. So, I wrote, and I wrote,

and I wrote. The silence was like a chamber of voices to a mad man. It was emotional turmoil, breaking me down from the inside out. It is very scary and dangerous to be mentally and emotionally unstable in prison; hopelessness is always just around the corner. I needed my strength to keep fighting…fighting feelings of worthlessness, fighting my failures, my anger, my regrets, and fighting my case. Every day was a battle to stay healthy and sane. I believed that I would one day get back to my children. Thoughts of how my children were doing, how they were feeling, what they might be thinking going through and the hope of getting back to them one day were my driving force. So, some type of communication was vital to me. But there was nothing. Nothing but silence.

"Dear lord, grant me the strength to change the things that I can and the courage to accept the things that I can't."

In 1999, Maraia was only a year and six months, too young to understand of course. The responsibility was on her mother to aid our communication. Years passed. Eventually, at the cost of my own sanity and self-destruction I stopped writing. I had done everything in **my power** to establish our connection and keep communication alive. I prayed that whenever Maraia does come of age that she will seek me out and hopefully get the answers she needs and hope that those answers are not too late to help her heal and move forward. Maraia was still my child and one day she would have questions about me. I hoped…

In the meantime, she would also be growing and developing as a young person. Her mental and emotional health is just as vital to her success as any other necessity-to luxury that she may have been enjoying in the process of her upbringing. But her mother's responsibility, (*that other parents' responsibility*) is the responsibility that no one wants to talk about. When it's most challenging for us as human beings to 'act' from the highest viewpoint of a difficult situation. In this case, what does it look like to act from the highest viewpoint of (**what is truly in the best interest of the child**) in the long run? I had already made my mistakes and had taken accountability for the terrible choices that took me out of the equation of my children's lives. Yet…**moving forward**, it wasn't about me.

Sins of the Mother *continued….*
In 1999, Amanda, the mother of Cayline was nowhere to be found. Five years had passed, by the time I was incarcerated. I searched for them everywhere I knew how. Me and my mom. But had Amanda searched for me as adamantly as I had searched for them? After all, the address and phone numbers to (my) whereabouts were unchanged at the time, especially my mother's address and phone number. Amanda and Cayline went of grid. And yes, I later found out that Amanda was fueled by misinformed from her mother about how I felt about Cayline. Cayline's grandmother had actually made up lies, that I didn't think Cayline was mine and that I didn't want her. Yet, is *misinformation* and Amanda's emotional wounded ness enough to excuse the responsibility of <u>seeking her</u> <u>own answers</u> for our

daughter's sake? After all, Amanda was an adult, she was also the (parent)? Wouldn't the mother of a child want her child to know their father? I mean, let's face it. I wasn't a drug addict. I wasn't a child molester. I wasn't a spousal nor child abuser. I wasn't a serial killer either. So, why wouldn't the mother of my child want to find me as bad as I wanted and needed to find them; especially, if she is doing everything from the standpoint of 'what's truly in the best interest of the child'? Is a father's responsibility or his role less or more important than that of the mother's? So, why is it a double standard in some women's mind's that it's okay to keep a child away from their father; once the relationship no longer serves (*the mother*), does her emotions and hurt feelings somehow excuse her from that part of her parental responsibility?

"*A relationship is not just one person's responsibility*"
-Thich Nhat Hanh

"The majority of wounds are created in the first 14 years of life, usually emanating from traumas experienced in the familiar environments of home, family, friends, and school. Being exposed to physical, mental, or emotional shock when the mind is at such an impressionable age results in the formation of what we might call crisis response wiring. This is an involuntary defense mechanism that the mind formulates in order to evade potential wounding that parallels the initial traumatic event. It seemingly rational tactic based on prevention. The problem is those years and even decades later, the old response wiring remains firmly in place. It is still fully operational and can be inadvertently triggered at any time. It can be activated by any number of things: a powerful emotional, a sequence of words, a particular smell, a piece of music, or even an entirely imagined scenario."

-On wounds and Trauma: as described by author: *Neil Kramer* in his book **'The Unfoldment'**.

Parenting Beyond Tragedy

Chapter 6: **Making Some Progress?**
Me & Maraia

I received my first letter from Maraia when she was fifteen going on sixteen. She did not know what to expect. She asked had I ever thought about her or cared that she even existed. I was in dismay, I had written many letters to her as a child. She had not received any of them. I told her to ask her mother, she did. She was told that they were stashed at her grandmother's house and so they were given to Maraia at that time. We shared a few more letters in between the time that I was moved to a closer facility on a hardship. We also shared a few phone calls at which time I was fortunate enough to have a conversation with her mother Tasha and her step-dad. I asked why they hadn't brought Maraia to see me over the years or have allowed or communication to go impeded for so long till now. Her step-dad replied that what Tasha does with her daughter is up to her, that he couldn't tell her how to parent her and that situation any different than Tasha could tell him what to do with him and his son's that are from a previous relationship. I disagreed, yet, I allowed him to express his truth on the matter without

conflict. When I asked Tasha, she was politely defensive about how the past is the past and I shouldn't be still tripping of what's already occurred. #Don't Cry over spilled milk? What! Where kids are concerned...

"Failing to act is also an action; it's an active choice."
-Damon L. Davis

Maraia came to visit me when she turned eighteen, here at The Denver Diagnostic and Reception Center maybe a fifteen-minute drive from where she lives. It was an awkward visit. There were so many things that she didn't understand, that she had questions about. As I answered many of her inquisitions I could sense that everything that I said was being filtered through the past eighteen years of what was never broken down nor explained to her while she was growing up. Her mother and step father took the parental approach of 'Though they had not bad mouthed me to my daughter over the years, they had not been proactive either, in giving her any information positive or otherwise about who I was so that Maraia could make up her own mind and have a better starting point of what she felt about me and our relationship. I asked Maraia, now that she is eighteen and has come to visit, had her mom said anything to her in regards to the events leading up to my incarceration she said all her mother said was that she told me not to do anything stupid…Hmmm, I guess that was all the effort (we) were worth back then.

"Roots are the foundation of the home. Roots, helps us discover who are. Family is the adhesive that holds it together from which a Kingdom can be built. The union of man and woman is the well of life; protect it, honor it with love and concentration so that succeeding generations can fell what it means to have balance, prosperity, longevity along this turbulent journey to peace." ~2010 Damon L. Davis

Well, Maraia has since had two children. I was never informed of their births from her. I have not received any pictures of my grandchildren, a boy and a girl. I have no idea what their names are. I believe my grandson's name is Azia (pronounced 'Ah-z-eye'). I'm almost certain that I've misspelled his name. I can't imagine how scary and confusing things must be for her. But she is a grown young woman now, and her decisions are her own.
#**The Price of Wisdom**

Me, Cayline & Amanda
I had been incarcerated for almost two years when I receive a letter from Trenton New Jersey. It was Amanda. There was a small photo of Cayline. The letter read: "Here is a picture of Cayline your daughter. She is smart and beautiful. Question, do you ever wonder about her? She deserves to know who you are. Is it true that you said that you don't want her, that you don't believe she yours? If you ever wonder about us, this is the address. She deserves to know her father."

I was elated and broken hearted at the same time. I was completely blown away when I got the letter. I was devastated. I read the letter in tears. I didn't eat any of the remaining meals served that day for chow. I remained in my cell till the next day. I was at Centennial Correctional Facility in a sixteen-man pod; all the cells were single man cells. I began writing a letter to Amanda about 2 a.m., detailing the events in my efforts to find her and Cayline after she left including the failed communication attempts with her mother in order to continue my visits with Cayline. I told her that all the things her mom said about me not wanting Cayline were lies; that I loved my daughter insanely and that I was crushed ever since she just disappeared without a trace. I also expressed how much I loved and respected her (Amanda) for keeping thoughts of me alive in the heart and mind of Cayline all this time by not brainwashing my daughter to believe that someone else was her father; for that alone, I had so much love, honor, and respect for Amanda. To her, my expression of these emotions was foreign, she had never felt any of those emotions and feelings from me let alone, ever heard me express them. Several letters later I received a phone number to call. Amanda said that the letters that I sent were so characteristically unfamiliar with her memory of me that she literally thought that she was corresponding with the wrong person. Had it not been for the slight familiarity in my voice and knowledge of certain key details that she knew; that only I'd know. She still, would have not believed she was speaking to the father of her child.

KARMA (lit. action) 1.) Any action—physical, verbal, or mental. 2.) Destiny, which is caused by past actions, mainly those of previous lives.

Well, right before another communicative travesty struck I was actually able to speak with my baby. It was a soul moving experience. Cayline spoke to me describing her friends at school. She described her best friend as being 'half chocolate' too (referring to the ethnicity of her friend). It was the cutest thing I ever heard spoken from a child's lips. My child.

The next opportunity I had to call the number was disconnected. Panic set in. I wrote frantic letters asking what happened, what's going on, is everything okay, did I do something wrong? A few letters in, I received a short
letter with another phone number. Amanda said that my case manager told her that I said that Cayline wasn't my daughter and that I was never getting out of prison so why is she even communicating with me. Devastated and angry, again, I found myself defending the truth against wicked lies. I was pissed and felt helpless, desperately clinging to the only lifeline I had to my baby girl. And people that I don't even know or care about were attacking me in area's they had no business tampering with. On top of that, Amanda went on to explain to me her and Cayline's living arrangements. That they were in Trenton New Jersey with Cayline's grandmother and she was the financial card holder. She said that her mother knew she was in contact with me and Amanda didn't cease the communication that she was going to cut them off financially. This argument had been going on since she first re-connected with me. It is also why the letters were so hit-and-miss and why she had to give me a different phone number. Amanda was a single mother who was doing okay for herself, but she was thinking of Cayline's future.

So, yes, you guessed it. Very shortly after, there was no longer a response to my letters and the phone number was disconnected. I didn't blame her. How could I. <u>It was definitely a decision made in the 'best' interest of the child wasn't it</u>? It didn't stop me from filling out the 'Angel Tree' forms for Cayline *(Angel Tree is a*

Christian service program that allows prisoners to send their kids free Christmas gifts every year up to certain ages). To my amazement these gifts were also rejected. I didn't find out until one day the company themselves wrote me a letter detailing their many failed attempts to deliver the gifts to Cayline; at one point even, hand delivering them to the doorstep at the resident. They were personally denied by Mrs. Purcell…Cayline's grandmother.

Eleven years later…I received my first letter from Cayline. It was one of the happiest and saddest days in my life; mainly, the saddest. She was asking questions that I had long since answered in the many letters that never reached her. Her words, each syllable, each individual letter was a Mike Tyson blow to my heart, my soul, my limbs, imagining how many nights she went to sleep not knowing if I loved her…not knowing if I was thinking of her…how many school days had she endured, how many lunches, field trips, show and tells…etc. I would have given my last breath just to hold her. The second letter Cayline sent me a necklace unaware that I could not have these types of personal items sent directly from the streets to prison. I dreaded how it would make her feel that I had to send it back. I wanted to send it anywhere but back to her, yet there wasn't anyone that I could trust that would keep it safe for me over time, so I was forced to send it back and even that was a task because I didn't have anyone I could count on for that. A Godsend of a friend, Lisa Phillips of Aurora Colorado answered the call. It was a shot in the dark; I hadn't heard anything from Lisa in a while our communication was on and off at times. So, when Cayline received the necklace back she took it as rejection which was far from what it really was. I explained why I couldn't have it but to a teenage girl who was tragically missing her father already for the first seventeen years of her life (*and still counting*) there was no reasoning in her mind. In Cayline's mind I was rejecting her, point blank. It was another major blow psychological for both of us and a major father and daughter bonding setback. We exchanged several letters after that. Cayline would send me matching envelopes and paper that had cute little puppies or kittens on them. She was more curious and worried how (I) was doing and what (I) was feeling, if I was safe and okay; always expressing how much she loved me. She mentioned that she is also planning to move from Jersey to Florida to be with her aunt and cousins down there. Our communication seemed consistent and going smoothly. Then all of a sudden it went silent… No letters, no answered phone calls. It seems like every time we start getting close, it's a trigger for her. Life, I imagined was moving forward for her in a positive way; college, a boyfriend maybe, other family, employment. And I was a distraction. Some years passed and then in came Florida hurricane season. I was worried sick. I still was unable to get in contact with Cayline to see if she was okay. It was strange. Eventually, I heard from my mom that Cayline and my brother periodically communicate on face book; nothing too extensive, just on major holidays and such. Yet there was no attempt to make a connect with me and no attempt from my brother to reach out to me and fill me in. In fact, I'm out the loop. I wish there was some way for me to be there for

Cayline. Or to know whether or not she even wants me to. **#Confused Heartbroken.**

Absent
(inspired by Lavie and my 1ˢᵗ grandson Malachi)

We woke up this morning in separate rooms in separate beds. I made mine you made yours. It's breakfast time. We put god first, our folded hands followed by a prayer verse.
You searched the cabinets for a meal to put your son's stomach first. I opened some oatmeal, peanut butter, and a granola bar because mine hurt.
My food was provided for by a jpay sent from Tony, my partner who I was raised with from the dirt. Yours was provided for by your sacrifice and hard work.

We both pay bills, but our dues are different.

There's no man at home and for you, I'm just gone. Alone, we've both moved on. Love doesn't live there anymore.

I've stuffed my bag with greens. You came home and dropped your bags on the floor. Where did we go?

"You", into the welcoming arms of your son; "Me", into the vacant seat on a bus. We haven't hugged in two decades...who are we?

Father and daughter

Pain. A great substitute for rage. A poor substitute for love estranged. You are succeeding at parenting. I've failed at the same. Countless birthdays missed, including the life births of a father's most precious beings, my three little darlings.

Abundant blessings.
Nevertheless,
We woke up this morning in separate rooms, in separate beds. I made my mine. You made yours. It's breakfast time. We put god first, our folded hands followed by a prayer verse, always hoping for the BEST, but never prepared for the *worst.*

You're a child at home raising children.

I'm in prison.

ABSENT.

Please, forgive me.

Me & Lavie, ***Good Dad, Bad Dad***
One of the most challenging issues I've struggled with over the years with all of my children as an incarcerated father, especially with my oldest daughter Lavie is the ability to show her that I love and support her, at the same time impart a sense of wisdom and guidance in her life. How can I? I've been absent most of her life. I know, it's foolish to even think that I could from my position. But what can I say…I'm a father nonetheless.

At twenty-three, Lavie is at a stage in her life where she feels that everyone who loves her and who is there to help her are against her. She takes everything as a personal attack on her ability to make good decisions. She clearly views her experiences through as a victim's stance. Lavie is acting out, taking a lot of her frustrations out on her grandmother. She is being highly disrespectful and even physically abusive toward her grandmother. This really upsets me. She doesn't know that I know about her behavior. When we speak on the phone she blames everything on her grandmother and her aunt. She never takes responsibility for her role in her struggles. Whenever I ask what's going on with her or give reflections from what she's told me of her own behavior and attitude; she immediately feels as though I'm against her and attacking her instead of supporting her. I want to just listen. Yet my parental instincts are eager to help, to save, to teach; especially as an absentee father. I feel unskillful and helpless at times because I understand how she feels to feel that no one understands her, especially those closest to her. Yet, her outbursts and many of her misperception of things is my fault. I failed her. She feels abandoned, unloved, and has a negative filter for her relationships. I've been in prison for twenty years of her life. It is not an excuse for her behavior. Yet, my absence is a key factor of why she feels the way she does. True, she is grown and is responsible for how she feels and how she chooses to respond to situations but how is she supposed to know how to work through those difficult thoughts, feelings, and emotions without the proper guidance, self-knowledge and life skills and most of all, without the love and support of her father?

It is difficult to wrap my emotional arms around her and give Lavie the warmth that she needs from a letter and a phone call; to show her that I love and care for her as well as impart to her that her grandmother is there to help her and her son; that she needs to respect her grandmother and her rules especially while she is living under her roof. She constantly pushes the right people away and the wrong people close.

I love Lavie and all my children dearly. Yet, at this point in her life she is struggling the most without my presence. I am learning as a dad to just listen; something that is entirely difficult to do as a parent from any position without wanting to offer some type of guidance; especially, after not being there for her for so many years. The emotional trauma has leaked into all parts of our lives, especially hers. Lavie and I are stronger and closer now, but our moments got way worse before they got any better. Here's a reflection of our struggle: *(A Phone call 5 years later…. between Lavie and I)*

"You don't know me! And I don't know you! You don't understand what it is for me to be out here and I don't know what you are going through in there! Nobody understands me! I am alone. I'm tired of being strong!" (My ears seem to go deaf for what feels longer than a few seconds). "I don't have anyone, you ruined my life! I wish you weren't my father! I think its best that we don't talk anymore! I shouldn't have answered this call! I don't want to talk to you as a matter of fact! - *(dial tone)*."
(Someone else is in line for the phone).

"Are you done, he asks?"

"Yeah."

"You sure?"

"Yeah man, I reply. It's Friday, I have to get ready for my shift." I bound up the stairs to my partner's cell. He was born in prison. He has never met his father. He doesn't have the luxury option of a phone call. He has never met nor felt the embrace of his mother. He has been incarcerated since he was 18 years old. He is 36. He has a son and a daughter. He has accomplished many things while in prison. We spend a few minutes in general conversation on that subject and a few details of my phone call. I want to tell my daughter about my friend William. But Lavie doesn't want encouragement. She doesn't want a pep talk. What's her love language I wonder? I could hear the desperation in her voice, but she could not hear the desperation in my mind to reach out to her nor feel the desperation in my heart, to hold her, to comfort her. So, I tell her that it's okay that everything will be alright. Wrong. She doesn't want to hear that. I believe that she just wanted her dad to listen to her.

Well, better luck next time I say to myself. Damn…a simple hug could've solved everything.
#GAVEIT2GOD

Chapter 7: **How did we get here?**

This is for my brother's
Yeah you! With that heat! That fire! The realest of 'em!
The ones who shed their tears in darkness
The ones whose hearts from the grind have been made
heartless

For the men enlisted in listless prison garments
Soul mates away from love and happiness

This is for my brother's, the realest of 'em
The ones who shed their tears in darkness
The ones whose hearts from the grind have been made
heartless

The ones whose roots have been cut off from their
children by grudges and nastiness
Family structures broken down
Lost in senseless madness
That stretch for miles & hours over countless distances
Yeah this is for my brother's
The realest of 'em
The ones who shed their tears in darkness
The ones whose hearts from the grind have been made
heartless

The ones with that heat! That fire!
Standing firm with a will of steel,
We become stone cutters
Shattering the pain crusted hearts of other's uplifting one
another

With knowledge & wisdom passed on from brother to
brother
Those who refuse to be smothered,

Grab-hold of your destiny! Strengthen your mind!
Discover yourself!
Guard well against the enemies that travel in stealth.

Yeah this is for my brothers, the realest of'em
The ones who shed their tears in darkness

The ones who hearts from the grind have been made
heartless

How did we get here?
More so,
The question is…how do we stop this,
This merry go round, this vicious cycle of hurt and
anguish?

The path of a conscious man has never been painless
So, complaining about matters of difficultly
Is futile, even aimless
Never have I known a warrior to emerge from the
battlefield; "Honorable, yet stainless."

Yeah this is for my brothers, the realest of'em
The ones with that heat, that fire!
The ones who shed their tears in darkness
The ones whose hearts from the grind have been made
heartless.

The time is now that I wipe my tears away,
Pray. Tighten up my boots. Walk out of my cell seeking
another victory out of today;

Because '**HOME**' is where I really want to be.

The Parenting Revelation of Ahmad Nelms

Parenting from behind prison walls can be very difficult and tricky at times. I have two children, my daughter Ahmiya Nelms and my son Tyree Howard-Nelms; our relationships have been two totally different experiences. Me and my son's relationship has been tight, but for all the wrong reasons. He has followed my footsteps into the gang life even being quoted into the same gang as I am. I think that makes him feel closer to me, like us have something in common.

I always tell him about the down falls of the gang life and how he's living, is not really living. I've told him that when you make mistakes in that life it can ruin many lives in an instant. I tell him to look at me as an example of what that life 'gives and takes'; to look at us even. My son is twenty-two years old and I've been in prison for twenty years! Also have a daughter. We haven't kept in touch like my son and I. My daughter and I have only communicated periodically. We were fortunate to have a visit after not seeing one another for over thirteen years. When we saw each other in that visit we were able to have a much-needed face to face conversation. I was able to express to her how sorry I am for failing her and not being there for her when she really needed me over the past twenty years and counting. I wanted her to know that I owed her so much more than what I was able to give her. I wanted her to know how proud I am of her; she's accomplished so much for herself on her own. She attends college, working full time and becoming the woman I'd always prayed she become. I was happy that I was able to finally express this to her face to face. It has been a struggle trying to convey my love and concerns for their wellbeing within the confines of prison hoping that things would turn out for the better despite my absence. I am grateful to God for the overall healthy fates of my children thus far. Though, my son's fate at this point isn't truly ideal as I would like, yet there is still time, I am prayerful. For now, Tyree is alive, well, and not in prison. There is great contrast between the lives of Ahmiya and Tyree. I attribute the differences in their lives and mind set to the fact that they had two different sets of values instilled in them due to the fact that they were raised by two separate mothers'; two different women with two different approaches to parenting under these circumstances. Ahmiya's mother acknowledged that all the odds were stacked against her, so she made sure that those odds didn't define her or become the reality of her and our child. While Tyree's mother allowed some of the same misfortunes and ideologies to plague my son's life and become his reality. Of course, it is not a simple task raising a child on any level, let alone as a single a mother; especially when the father of those children is in prison with a life sentence to boot. What is a mother to do? The grace of God's covers us and as human beings we can only give what we have within ourselves. So, it's up to us to put forth the energy necessary for us to evolve.

As for my son Tyree, I've tried to influence my son to do something different with his life, but it is hard to tell someone what 'not' to do when all they know of you is the gangland legend, the person that you are telling him 'not' to be. And it is also easy the mothers to forget how vital a positive relationship with the father of the children is, even when he is in prison; something of a positive influence is better than none at all. And with that, 'parenting beyond tragedy' there needs to be more care of what's said about the father, (good or bad) in the presence of the children; left up to interpretation the children filter how they please, maybe glorifying attributes they shouldn't and condemning characteristics and attributes they should admire.

LIFE

I never knew what life was until I was sentenced to life.

I never knew what life was until I missed my daughter's entire life.

I never knew what life was until my sister lost her life and I couldn't go to the funeral because I had life.

Some say that life is too short, but that's not true. Life is too long especially if you make the wrong decisions.

Many people have judged me during my life without knowing what it's been like to live my life. For many years I've blamed everyone else for the mistakes I've made in my life. But today I know no matter what how young I was I'm responsible for all my mistakes I've made in my life.

And today, all I want to do is to help the kids not make the mistakes that I've made in my life. And now I understand LIFE.

And ALL I want is to one day, have a *LIFE*.

"Life" by Ahmad Nelms

Triumph over tragedy
Ahmad Nelms; a father, life coach, mentor and loyal friend. 'If I had to use one word to describe him.' **"RESILENCE."**

"Who you are in life is not found in your skill, Talent, your ability, or your career, it's found in your character." - **ETHICS 101, John C. Maxwell**

William S. Graham's Parenting Timeline
"If there is not a community for you, young man…make it for yourself." -Paul Goodman

Truthful
I know this might sound strange to many people, but I was preparing to be a father at the age 9 years old. I can hear you saying (what!) right now, but it's true. More importantly, the reason why I found myself contemplating fatherhood at such an early age was for selfish reasons. I wanted to show my dead-beat dad I could be a better father than he was.

I remember having a constant burn in the pit of my chest for him. Even when someone would mention his name, I would go off like a firework show. I hated him that much. But here's the kicker, I hated a ghost. I've never met my father, not one single time.

I was a kid with no past, forced to roam the earth trapped in a paradox of abandonment. Another kid who shared my pain in this paradox was my baby brother Calvin. The brother I practically raised myself. One day, my baby brother and I were walking home from school and I bent

down to tie his shoe strings. I still remember his tiny little voice. "William, do we have a daddy?"
I looked puzzled. "Nah, we don't got no daddy."
"Where did we come from if we don't got no dad?"

I lied to him with a straight face. "We were born without a dad." He was only seven years old, but that didn't stop Calvin from staring at me like a damn fool. His face read (do you think I'm that stupid?). He didn't question me on it any further, probably because he was just like me, he didn't want to hear the real answer. The real answer was that our father didn't give a damn about the kids he brought into this world.

Focused
Around the age of 15 years old, it's safe to say my efforts toward fatherhood had settled down. I told myself I would just be the best big brother I could be. By now, I had already dropped out of school, not a smart move, seeing how important education is for everyone. My adopted aunt begged me to enroll in Job Corp, since I was banned from 70% of the schools in Carolina. I granted her wish one week before I turned 16 years old. My aunts' older son Josh, who I revered as a father figure supported my dreams and also put up with a lot of my non-sense. He would always give me these power speeches on how important issues in life are what

actually give us purpose. If I had to describe him in one word, (focused) would be that word. I wish I had focus when I was at Job Corp. I didn't do anything except chase tail, and gang bang. I was trying to put up a solid front. I promised my aunt over the phone that I would get my grades, which was more for her than me. It wasn't long before I found myself kicked out of a Job Corp like an evicted tenant. I went back home with a wagon full of shame, and disappointment in my heart. My aunt couldn't even look me in my eyes. With two feet out the door, I was led by my pride, telling myself, "I don't care what anyone thinks, I'm me."

At the age of seventeen, I got a call from my older brother who was stationed at Fort Carson in Colorado Springs, CO. The heartfelt conversations led to an invitation to come join him for about three months out in Colorado. I told myself I could use a vacation, so I quickly obliged his offer.

Snow…I looked out the window to see the ground was covered with snow. That was the first time I had actually seen and felt snow. Anyway, I had to give you guys a catch-up reel of my life before I had kids. Out here acting mannish in Colorado, it didn't take me long to become a father, two different women, my two children six months apart (#dog's life).

Joyful
I remember being very joyful when I heard the news of my first and second child on the way. I use to tell my

friends, having kids aren't nothing to be afraid of, disappointing kids is something to be afraid of. Compassionate and…unaware, I believe as father's we find ourselves nervous about having kids because it's like a test we'll never have all the right answers for. We are unprepared in multiple aspects. Even I was caught off guard when the news of my future legacy would be arriving in nine short months. I remember thinking the following things in no certain order:

- I hope don't mess these kids up
- What if they don't like me?
- So, what if they don't like, I'm daddy, that's the law!
- Will they look at me? (Be careful with that subject)
- How will they act?
- This can't be as hard as people say it is, can it?
- I need to make some money
- I need to get a better job
- I got a warrant out for my arrest, I can't get a job
- I need some quick money now!

With that kind of pressure cooking inside my head, it didn't take me long to start doing unlawful acts to get money. I was robbing at night, and covering up my tracks with a daily burger gig I had. I thought I was so clever, unaware of my genius actions, having no back up plan. Not too add, I told myself I wouldn't get sucked into this life of crime once my kids were brought to my attention. (I lied) …I found myself deeper than ever. I had a huge heart, but I wasn't being smart. "Some of the worst things are done with the greatest intentions."

Serious

As you could have guessed, seeing how my actions were not the most dapper after only two years of causing hell I found myself sitting in the El Paso County Jail. I faced a life sentence for my criminal activity, thirty-one counts of aggravated robbery, nine counts of kidnapping, and a lot of other things that involved taking money from people. My lawyer said to me, "Mr. Graham, you're facing a lot of time." As I stared into his eyes I noticed that he was more scared than I was.

While in the county jail, my daughter Jamaica and my son Cyprese were brought into this world. I felt like I could die. I remember sitting on my bed with a fistful of tears. I had officially broken my childhood promise to myself. My kids would not be born into this world without their fathers' face here to embrace them … (they were). I brushed my teeth the next morning, and walked directly up to this guy and punched him in the face. I was mad at the world. When I tell you that I was lost man it's not a joke. They say pride go before the fall … they weren't lying. I received 137-year sentence that later, by the grace of God, got reduced to 72 years. These are my sins… sins of dropping the ball-hard where my children are concerned. Yes, I fell distinctively short of my parental responsibilities. I own every bit of my choices and take full accountability for all of my life and the role

I failed to play thus far in my children's lives. Traditionally, 'parenting' consists of two people, where one's lack of responsibility ends the other surely begins, 'picks up', and then never ends'. As I write this passage,

118

fifteen years of incarceration have passed between me and my children, yet I am still a father.

So, to highlight some of the ugly, often hidden emotions, those that linger in the hearts of the mothers of my children, ponder this…I didn't see my kids for maybe 13 years out of the 15 years I've been in prison. The excuse got very old, which was, "I'm working, I just don't have time to bring your child up there." This occurred year after year as if I was stupid or something. I knew what it was and so did they. I was being replaced by a substitute dad. No one wanted to address the underlining factors, so we danced around the truth. The truth was, like many spiteful women who use the child as a bargaining chip, they longed to cause me pain. (Kick a man while he's down was the name of the game). If what I've just said isn't true, then explain the epidemic which sweeps the country, why so many men inside the prison system don't see their children? There's not that much working in the world. Then after you've spent all but a few dollars of your twelve-dollar state pay to talk on the phone to your children and ask your kids mom to put something on the phone to extend the conversation, she says, "I'm broke!" She's not broke, but what is still broke (and I can assure you that it has nothing to do with our kids) is her heart, believe that! And she'll let that be the reason that our child will suffer every time, if I'm not the one providing for the means of communication & connection, she'll be the last person to. Yet, this is what's accepted by society from the other parent. Let's get real when addressing these issues, and stop putting powdered sugar on it.

Keepsake

This past year or so we've been blessed with more frequent communication and interactions due to the fact that I am now, a published author of six books and counting.

Recently, my son and I were discussing gang affiliation. I told Cyprese, "You don't need a gang when you have me!" Saying those words to him almost made me cry (because that's what I wanted my father to come tell me thirty-five years ago). My son is like a feline (a Leo) that watches what you do and wonders if he should eat you or make you pet him.

Jamaica …my daughter is like a wild rose that grows where and how it wants. If you try to make her do something she does not like, she'll make you pay for wasting her time.

Impact

With my last salute to this subject, I will agree with the world that parenting is a full-time job that only a few of us excel at. I'm not one of the great ones, but I try each and every day to better myself in every aspect, hoping

that my examples of love will reflect my actions of love and resonate in the hearts of my children and all those that I care about. Of course, when we sleep on parenting is when the bad things happen.

Someone once told me a great father is hard to find, if he disciplines you too much you'll say that he's too harsh on you. And if you don't get any discipline you'll say that he didn't care for you. And if that's too much pressure, just simply look at those times as a moment to be with the man you call…your father.

My name is William S. Graham and my fatherhood has no bounds. To all my kids, the message is simple, "I love you all and I'm here for you."

William is a father that any child would be proud to call dad, A son that any parent would be filled with pride over, A man that any woman would be proud to call husband, A man that any man would be proud to call brother, A man that any stranger would be proud to call friend. Mr. Graham is a man that any neighbor would feel safe to call neighbor, A gem to human kind, a true value to himself and any community he is a part of; A servant leader (-*William S. Graham, 'Profound, Opinionated, Faithful, Assertive.)'*

"*Triumph over Tragedy.*"

After all, … "A man who honors God privately will show it by making good decisions publicly." **-Edwin Louis Cole**

William S. Graham author of:
Leave the Door Open
Get Off the Tricycle
The Locksmith of Love
Forty Degrees of Love
A Diamond Bond & Fifty Degrees of Love
Co-author of:
God Can and God Will
Difference between a Queen and a Thot
Stir
A New life

Parenting Beyond Tragedy

<u>Chapter 8</u>: **Beyond Tragedy** (*Open Conversation*)
When I was initially inspired to write this book, I was pained from the perspective of my own situation. I also found out that many incarcerated men have or were experiencing the same issues. I mean, I was tripping on how diverse the subject was. Over the years I've spoken with men from all ethnicities, cultural back grounds, and social economic status. There were different experiences on family, money, and life in general. Yet, we all shared the same, if not, very similar experiences when it came to the mothers of our children. It was seemingly always the same scenario. In almost every case the men were either villainized, made absent, alienated, or minimized in the lives of their children by the mothers of their children. No matter how much effort was put into trying to communicate with the children, no matter how much the father put into making amends, taking accountability for his mistakes, nor how much the father's expressed their love and the significance of maintaining the connection with his children, no matter how many letters were written, arts & crafts sent, no matter how many Angel Tree gifts received or rejected, no matter how many

failed phone calls attempted, the fathers' effort was always met with disdain and or worse…with no response at all. As time passes, one is left to ponder…What the difference is between the fathers who do care and the men that don't? And why it seems that the scales are tipped in favor of those many individuals who have the self-centered, self-absorbed attitudes? What's the attraction to the men that say, "F- it, I'm in prison, the kids will be fine," vs. the father's that wants to salvage some type of relationship with his children if the end the relationships with the children are still distant and damaged? Then, why bother to care at all?

For example:
Over a course of twenty years, I've listened to and observed countless men candidly maintaining their psychological positions all the while enjoying the spoils of visits, canteen, j-pay's, and more phone time than they know what to do with for years on end from baby momma's and ex-wives. I know men personally who would blow hundreds of dollars on the poker table rather

than send it to their children, write a letter, get involved in the 'read to the children' program.
Ironically, there are two stigmas here. It seems that these absentee fathers aren't judged the same by their baby mommas' as the men who actually (do) care and have taken full accountability of their lives, their mistakes and the affects that their bad decisions have had upon their children lives.

Seemingly, the men with the 'F-it' attitudes are the ones whose love and affection seem to be tirelessly sought after by the children when they come of age. Even the women in this type of scenario, the baby mother's themselves seem to be caught in a cycle of control and approval from the fathers as well. From this perspective, men with women in those positions live like kings in the penitentiary (on the penitentiary scale that is). When in all actuality, these men couldn't care less about what's going on with their children or the baby mammas for that matter. Nevertheless, the attraction to the absentee father is strong and they seem to be the ones winning.

I find it interesting, why some women with incarcerated baby daddies take this position, especially when so many baby mommas put themselves on a pedestal by taking the opportunity when a man goes to prison to bash their baby daddy on his mistakes and responsibilities as a parent; as if parenting was exclusive to just *one* parent.

However, with this attitude as it relates to the women 'who for whatever reason' stick by the men who only care about themselves. I wonder if there is some trauma that they themselves are masking? Maybe the men themselves have the right idea? Maybe it is a better survival option like 'living in the moment' that gets them through than the toll it may take on their mental health if they worried and actually cared about what was happening at home? Maybe this is something that the mothers of their children understand and empathize with? So, they stick with them rather than abandoning them?

The children, at the beginning, are often times too young to realize that they are caught up in the same vicious cycle of mental and emotional control patterns as their mother. And when they do come of age they struggle with feelings of abandonment, guilt, shame, and rejection. Children too often blame themselves for their father's absence. Despite the lack emotional intelligence to navigate their feelings, the anger and confusion is enough of a driving force for them to continue seeking closure and their father's approval long after his rejection is obvious. Yet, the effects of this level of emotional residue on a child can take an entire lifetime to unravel. And it usually does.

Weighing the Scales

Why, in most relationships when things go sour the woman always feels like she has full ownership over the children? Women are always saying things like, "I'll take the children and back to my mammas house or leave the state. etc. etc." I've always tripped off of that expression whenever I hear it or see it in movies. It's crazy because it seems embedded so far back in our culture. You could dang near pop in a movie from every century and see the recurring theme of that statement. I've often wondered what is going thru a woman's mind whenever they make that statement. Clearly, women don't make children by themselves. Yet, it seems to be the (go to) in bitter situations involving children, as if taking the child away from the father will turn out to be in the best interest of a child in the long run.

I watched the movie 'Equalizer 2' with Denzel. There was a scene at the very beginning about a father kidnapping his child from the mother, the actor in the scene (Denzel's character) said, "that it was a violent and abusive act to take a child from its mother." Yet, it is funny that-that is never the case when a mother acts in similar fashion toward the father, taking the children in all vindictiveness…

I recently watched the movie "Hands of Stone" about the great boxer Roberto Duran. The first time he and his wife got into what seemed as though it was a relationship ending dispute his wife retorted, "I am taking the kids!"

Just hearing that type of outburst in real life or on TV is a trigger for me. It is an extremely selfish statement. Yet, many women seem to feel entitled to say and do at the first sign of trouble in a relationship. But why? I believe they waste no time weaponizing the children because they know that in the event things end up in court that the courts will further empower their vindictive position. More often than not thing s seem geared to go their way. It's sad but true, you rarely see instances where women are called to account for their selfish acts, (their roles etc.) in bitter custody battles and divorces cases etc. The proceedings always seem to focus on the fault and or responsibility of the father. Of course, not always, but if we were to put it on a scale the disparity would be apparent.

Take the Brad Pitt and Angelina Jolie situation for example, until their recent divorce you never heard of

Brad Pitt not being a great father and provider for his children. Yes, I'm sure it is a lot more to the story than what we see or read in the media but what we do see and read from Angelina is very accusatory negative toward Mr. Pitt. He has not taken the same vindictive approach. He is just now being allowed to see his children. Who gave Angelina sole custody/ ownership in the first place? Where is the equality there? They're both equally successful and influential. Why, were all the cards seemingly, immediately placed in the mother's favor?

And yet still, the even greater focus is that the kids are still the ones impacted the most. The children even among the wealthy have to adjust the same; tragedy makes no distinction of wealth, social status or anything else. The bottom line is "What's in the best possible interest of the children," should positively bind both parents to a higher standard especially in times of tragedy, where the call of duty and need for support for the children is even higher.

As in the instances of William, Ahmad, and I who have made greater mistakes than a failed marriage. In addition to taking responsibility for our crimes and being fully accountable for ourselves. We've turned our lives around, attaining personal success and positively impacting the lives of countless others as life mentors within the Department of Corrections. We have also become greater examples for our families, especially our children. Wisdom from our mistakes that they can grow from. But where are the women who can say the same who will own up to their responsibility and claim their accountability for not holding up their end knowing that they could have done more or something very different to ensure the best possible outcome in terms of promoting communication and connection via letters, visits, phone calls etc. between father and child? The father who is in prison is unable to fully control the means of communication and interaction with his children. That is solely in the control of the mother especially when the children are not yet of age.

I can hear some of the women reading this now saying, "I did what I was supposed to do, don't judge me, you are the one who went to prison who are you to judge me! You left us!" True, men in my position have made our choices. Yet 'judging us' is exactly what some women do when the man messes up. They impede upon the child-father relationship or do nothing at all to enrich it. Even more ironic, most baby mommas want us men to stay in that (very moment of guilt and shame forever). As if they expect us to live the rest of our lives making it up to (them). Let alone, the children.

"Judge not lest ye be judged."-Jesus.

Well, how would it sound (if) we men said the same; that we did our best with what we had (meaning 'the mothers' of our children)? Because as the saying goes, "One can do bad all by themselves." As many women have said- just that. That they can do bad all by themselves. If the man that they're currently with is not producing, pulling his weight so to speak; doing bad. Then why stay with him? So likewise, as the father of the child, if he's failed and have ended up in prison then his failure is also your failure. (If) we are looking through the lens of (that kind of judgment) as so many women have for so long with men in many of life's situations, let alone an incarcerated absentee father. My question to women who fit this category, those that ride the high horse in these matters is that: 'If your man, your baby father was so important to you, what was your prevention strategy? Where was your voice, your presence? Why so much flack (after the fact), if family values and the (dad's influence) is so important? Why not express all that fight and concern beforehand?

How much did you truly value the father in the first place if you did nothing at all?' Or was it just, all about the absence of the (potential monetary support) he would have provided that concerns you the most? Those are my questions for all women, not just ones whose baby daddies are or have been incarcerated. Why is, 'taking the kids' always the go to? Why keep a man's children from him? Why impede upon the growth of their relationship? Why do we all of a sudden feel the need to release ourselves from that other part of responsibility that would hold things together, in terms of the child-parent connection? I mean, please forgive me, but if I was a child who could step back and view things objectively I don't think I'd see or feel much motherly warmth here.

Remember, these are just impromptu questions to spark a much needed in depth conversation. If you are feeling triggered by anything you are reading, it's okay. Maybe it's time to self-reflect, to do some real introspection into the knee jerk thinking patterns of 'self-absorbing denial' that you were accustomed believing in so much? Side note: Feelings do not constitute nor validate truth.

Of course, no one human being is responsible for another human beings' behavior. Yet, in a relationship situation as in co-parenting, there is a sense of teamwork and personal responsibility that each person should bear. Especially, when there is tension, heartbreak, and tragedy where children are concerned. Both Parties need to step up. From a male's perspective that doesn't happen much. It is usually, the man who, by some double-standard in society, is expected to take the high road in most cases.

You know, "You made the mistakes etc., (you) hurt me
etc., so (you) man up and get over it. Take responsibility.
Be accountable and do what's right." While the women
on the other hand get to sit over their arms crossed,
finger-pointed at the man on their re-enforced, society
conditioned, self-righteous high horse; well-placed, sense
of security, feeling that they get a pass whenever they
can't get over their emotions simply because (by society
& scientific standards) 'their emotional by nature'. These
constructs that we've adopted as 'the norm' into our
family dynamic, daily behaviors, and interactions with
one another is by my observation and my experience,
unhealthy. Emotionally and psychologically what makes
this behavior healthy? If one person is always expected to
bear the brunt weight of all the disputes in a relationship,
a friendship or whatever simply because of his or her
gender where is the balance and harmony in that?
Furthermore, what are we really saying here?

Once a relationship is dissolved. Yet, depending on how
that relationship ended (in terms of connection and
communication with the biological father) to go down
with the ship. As the saying goes, "Hell hath no fury like
a woman scorned."

Communication failure is a subtle process. Not always,
but sometimes there are a melee of signs and
circumstances that reveal evidence of dilemma before the
actual tragedy of your man taking penitentiary chances.
There had to be some type of knowledge, or dialog that
suggested mental and emotional anguish. As they say in
criminal justice, "Guilty by association." I'm just
saying…Especially when two people have children

together things had to have been good at some point before falling apart, right? Of course, there are many exceptions to the scenario (one night stands for instance), but you understand what I'm getting at. It's sad, but a true reality for me and Maraia's mother. The re-occurring theme was that when things were great between me and Tasha we were a team. Yet, the moment things got challenging I was on my own. It is crazy the things you don't see when you're in love with someone with the world on your shoulders. Funny thing is…is that I don't regret loving her the way I did. I don't blame her for anything. We were young. We were kids. And I haven't met a kid yet, that wouldn't mess-off a million dollars if left to their own faculties on how to spend it. Love is like that even when it hits you 'so profoundly' at a young age.

I read somewhere that said, *"A relationship is not an opportunity but a sweet responsibility."* The raw reality with some relationships, is that most of us see our relationship as an opportunity. And therefore, the interplay of the relationship is merely a system of controls. A game of manipulation of who will benefit the most from their excertion of power over the other. Rather than the aim of strengthening the bond and deepening one's connection.

The Elaborate Drama *(the ugly truth)*
What would the parent-child connection look like if each of the incarcerated fathers had a million dollars that the Department of Corrections could not touch, yet, the fathers had access to; how would the mothers of the children have responded then? What would the level of

communication look like between the parents themselves? Even more intriguing, how much more open would the mothers of our children have been in taking on a proactive, less judgmental, and more forgiving role, rather than being resistive and indifferent?

One would have to ask, is it really about the absence of fathers' presence and influence or is it about the absence of monetary value and benefit that the father would have provided had he not been in prison?

I've yet to see a father being taken to court for not spending enough time with his children. I've yet to see a mother file for 'Time & Love Support' over child support. I mean let's be real, in most cases, child support translates as baby momma support. The child is usually the last thing on her of mind in moments of intense emotions when the bond between the two parents has been damaged. This predominate attitude is a societal pattern, a double standard if you will, that has to be broken. #Weaponizing The Children.

Society norms have diminished the presence of the father and emasculated his role and broken it down to monetary value. Is not the human warmth of the father the same as the mother? What type of attitude or mindset does it take to want to assassinate the idea of the father in the mind of his child?

In extreme cases when you have a father that wants nothing to do with his children or he himself is wretched, vile, and his behavior poses an imminent threat to the child; then at all cost the child must be protected. But even in such cases, at some point with due diligence when the (child is of age), sound mind, and in a position of safety and supervision; by all means, let the child decide what kind of relationship it will be, if he or she wants nothing to do with him, so be it. This is the high road of fairness at its extreme of 'what's in the best interest of the child in the long run. But to suddenly severe that opportunity for a rapport and or relationship between parent and child based on what the mother's opinion or how she feels about the man is completely selfish at its core (even in extreme circumstances such as described above). So how much more is it frowned upon when the father is the complete opposite of that? A father who is indeed loving, caring, and compassionate and wants to be in his child's life; Yet has made human mistakes no different than any other man or woman on this earth. Is he not worthy of a second chance, a rapport and relationship with his children? Is he not worthy of forgiveness…the same as any parent, say 'a mother' or any other adult who has made mistakes in their lives?

"If he hath wisdom, let him impart it. Especially to his own children. Be the pathway, be not the one who impedes upon it." **-Damon L. Davis 2021**

"If you for give men their trespasses, your heavenly father will also forgive you. But if you do not forgive men their trespasses, neither will your heavenly father forgive your trespasses." Matthew 6:14-15

Epilogue:

Prayer St. Francis of Assisi
Lord, make me an instrument of your peace.
Where there is hatred let me sow love.
Where there is injury, pardon.
Where there is darkness, light.
O' Divine Master grant that I may
Not so much seek to be consoled, as to console.
To be understood as to understand.
To be loved as to love.
For is in giving that we receive.
It is in pardoning that we are pardoned.
And it is in dying that we are born to eternal life.

Amen.

Parenting Beyond Tragedy

Divine intervention
During the actual transcribing of this book, *miraculously!*
Me, Lavie, and my grandson Malachi had our first ever,
visit! And I also received a long-awaited letter and
picture from Cayline!

The letter reads:
September 10ᵗʰ 2019
Hello dad,
I don't even know where to start… I'm sorry I
disappeared for so long. I don't know if you know
yet, but nan passed away January 13ᵗʰ 2018. I
completely lost myself for so a long time after
that it was hard to watch her pass the way she
did. I can't say sorry enough for abandoning you.
I hope you don't hate me. I heard you published a
book. I haven't got the chance to purchase it yet
but I am so proud
of you. I hope you're doing well and to hear back
from you. Sal and my mom are doing okay, Sal got
shoulder surgery and my mom had an accident
and she basically tore her ACL but she is doing
good and is going to recover. I recently have lost

a lot of friends this past may people that I thought cared about me but did not. I have a boyfriend as well named Joan, sadly he lives in Barton but he is a wonderful person and he encouraged me to write you. I was scared to write you because I thought you wouldn't want to hear from me after how our last convo' went. I also work at FedEx which kicks my ass. I start at 3:30 a.m. and finish at 8 a.m. So, the shifts are hard but it's good pay so I'm trying to push through. I 've been having a lot of issues with my mental health but I 'm trying to push through. Sorry, I am still a terrible writer. And my hand writing is so ugly. Ha-ha. ha, but hopefully its readable. Have a wonderful day and I love you!

Love Cayline xoxo

P.S. here's a photo's you might like!

<u>Recommended Reading</u>

The Greatest Salesman in The World by Og Mandino

Voices in The Cellar by Damon L. Davis

Hurt People…Hurt People by William S Graham

Failing Forward by John C. Maxwell

The Speed of Trust by Stephen M. R. Covey

As A Man Thinketh by James Allen

Master key to Wealth by Dr. Joseph Murphy

A Warrior of The Light by Paulo Coehlo

Everyone communicates few connect by John C. Maxwell

Parenting Beyond Tragedy

About This Book

Parenting Beyond Tragedy is a male perspective on co-parenting through the hardships of incarceration. It is about the importance of maintaining some sort of viable connection between the biological father and his children in spite the conditions of LIFE inside or outside the prison walls. There is a vital importance of having (some) connection and influence from the father, in a child's life verses (none at all). When it comes to parental disputes, co-parenting and the like the statement is: "Do what's in the BEST interest of the children." As a family unit (however fractured) we should act from the highest viewpoint of that statement.

Well-known Self-Help author William S. Graham and Life coach-gang prevention and Addiction mentor Ahmad Nelms share their experiences.

Parenting Beyond Tragedy

Damon L. Davis

Parenting Beyond Tragedy